Advance Prai

"I love this book! Aleta's wise and wonderful words ~~~~ ~~~~ ~~~~ .o a
new understanding and deep awareness. She has shown me that release and renewal are essential parts of growth."

—Carolyn Murphy, Estée Lauder spokeswoman,
supermodel, actress, and mother

"It is a pleasure to read a book that reaffirms the strength of women, at
any age. In her life and in her work, Aleta St. James inspires us to live
our dreams, and reminds us that there are no boundaries to desire."

—Joan Lunden, TV journalist and author

"Aleta St. James and her work have put into balance forces in my life
that I thought could never be balanced. She has made me less afraid
to look at the darkness because she has shown me it is the way to the
light."   —Austin Pendleton, actor, writer, director

"Aleta St. James is living proof that you can not only live your own
dreams, but that you can live in such a way as to inspire, empower,
and contribute to the dreams of others. Both her book and her life
are wonderful achievements."

—Jonny Bowden, MA, CN, CNS, nutritionist,
author, lecturer, and life coach

"Aleta St. James's abundant charm and worldly knowledge leaps
from every page of *Life Shift*. Aleta presents complex concepts in a
concise, easy to assimilate manner, leaving the reader with the tools
for real and significant change."

—Todd Oldham, designer

LIFE ✦ SHIFT

Let Go and Live Your Dream

ALETA ST. JAMES

A Fireside Book

PUBLISHED BY SIMON & SCHUSTER

NEW YORK   LONDON   TORONTO   SYDNEY

FIRESIDE
Rockefeller Center
1230 Avenue of the Americas
New York, NY 10020

The names and identifying characteristics of certain individuals
referenced in this book have been changed.

This Fireside Edition 2006

FIRESIDE and colophon are registered trademarks of Simon & Schuster, Inc.

For information regarding special discounts for bulk purchases,
please contact Simon & Schuster Special Sales at
1-800-456-6798 or business@simonandschuster.com.

Designed by Ruth Lee Mui

Manufactured in the United States of America

1   3   5   7   9   10   8   6   4   2

Library of Congress Cataloging-in-Publication Data is available.

ISBN-13: 978-0-7432-7692-4

ISBN-13: 978-0-7432-8187-4 (Pbk.)

For Gian and Francesca, the children I always wanted to have. And for my parents, who have been the best support team any daughter could ask for— you are my rock, a constant source of strength and inspiration.

CONTENTS

INTRODUCTION

No dream is too big. You just have to become the person the dream challenges you to be.

November 9, 2004, New York City

It was an early Tuesday morning, just three days before my fifty-seventh birthday, and I awoke knowing that I would finally realize my deepest dream: to have children.

I had been a good soldier: My doctors had been surprised that despite my age, I had had a model pregnancy. I had kept my sense of humor intact with my onward-and-upward attitude as I faced one difficulty after another, remaining patient through endless sonograms and fetal stress tests, experiencing horrendous morning sickness and relentless sciatic pain. But this morning, for the first time, I felt a profound sense of unease: I was emotionally unhinged and my body couldn't stop shaking.

My scheduled C-section was just a few hours away. Mentally I knew I was in great hands, but my body seemed to know it was going under the knife. It recognized how frightened I was even better than my head or heart did. Where was my faith when I needed it most?

Some people said I was nutty trying to get pregnant in my sixth decade, but I had a very different perspective. My grandmother Nicoletta *had given birth to my mother, the last of thirteen children, at the age of fifty-four, and I felt I could physically have a baby at this same age. I had finally met someone I wanted to settle down with. He was younger than I was and eager to start a family. I knew in my heart that over the years I had acquired a tremendous amount of wisdom, love, and compassion, and it was my great desire to share everything I had learned and raise a family. Physically, I was in great shape: People regularly told me I looked fifteen years younger than my age, and I felt healthy, vibrant, and alive.*

Even though I had worked as an emotional healer and life coach for twenty-five years, in my quest to get pregnant, I took nothing for granted and left no stone unturned. I traveled the world, working with famous shamans in Peru and participating in fertility rituals in the Hindu temples of southern India. I meditated, ate right, exercised, and strove to be emotionally and spiritually balanced. Three miscarriages and a relationship breakup later, I was forced to regroup. Instead of packing it in, I decided to become pregnant through in vitro fertilization. It took three years, and I had to overcome many obstacles, but I would fulfill my deep desire to become a mother.

On that fateful November morning, my dear friend Arthur, whom I'd known for twenty-six years, accompanied me into a taxi. As we sped along, he reached for my hand and gave me a reassuring touch. The driver dropped us in front of the hospital entrance and enthusiastically asked, "Are you the fifty-seven-year-old woman on the front cover of the Daily News *who's giving birth to twins?" Feeling like I was in someone else's movie, I nodded yes. The driver smiled and refused to take any payment for the cab ride, insisting that he was now part of the historic event.*

Once in the hospital, I was quickly whisked away to an operating room. As the anesthesia was taking effect, my friend Rita arrived, flying in from San Francisco to be by my side. Through her white surgical mask she said to me, "Eighteen years ago, I promised you that if you were ever to have children, I would be here, and here I am." Had the seed of this dream been growing that long?

Introduction

As my legs became increasingly numb, I enjoyed, for the first time in months, the absence of any sciatic pain. When my obstetrician, Dr. Scher, smiled down at me with his kind, reassuring enthusiasm that had meant so much to me throughout my quest to have children and asked, "Are you ready, Aleta?" in his charming South African accent, I cheerfully replied, "I couldn't be more ready!"

Before I knew it, I felt a tugging pressure and heard the first cries of my daughter, Francesca. Tears of joy rolled down my face as they lifted her up for me to see. My son, Gian, greeted the world one minute later with his own exuberant wailing, which rose over Rita and Arthur's play-by-play. "It's so amazing, Aleta! You have two gorgeous children!" The moment when I first laid eyes on them, I knew I was experiencing a miracle.

Much to my surprise, my story spread in the media like wildfire, creating a buzz here and in countries as far away as China, Turkey, India, and the Philippines. I heard from friends I hadn't spoken to in years, as well as perfect strangers: parents and children, elderly people and college students, and even a group of third graders from the Bronx who made cards congratulating me and the babies. For many, my story was a source of hope. People were inspired by the fact that I refused to give up, overcame the odds, and fulfilled my deepest dreams.

*Y*ou have an extraordinary dream as well—one that others may think is unattainable. You may see glimpses of it when you look in the mirror and are pleasantly surprised at what you see. You may feel its touch when you hold something dear from your past. You may even hear a whisper of it when you first wake up in the morning and approach a new day.

Like some of my clients, you may be unaware of what you really want out of life. Some of the people I work with seem to have it all—a lovely home, a family, wealth, prestige in the community, a career—and yet they are not deeply happy. Or, you may know what you want but feel frustrated that you cannot make this dream happen or manage one more change in your too-hectic life. Worse, your true self may seem unreachable because you've lost the desire to dream.

The good news is that you can get your desire back! I'm here to tell you that your dreams *are* attainable, that there is no such thing as an impossible dream. The secret is to reconnect with your intrinsically feminine ability to manifest desires. By redeveloping this ability, you absolutely can accomplish whatever you are supposed to do in this world.

Whether you find yourself a successful career woman, supermom, or single woman out on her own, the struggle to achieve excellence, be everything to everyone, *and* attain a level of personal/professional perfection has probably left you longing for your childhood days or (gasp!) your mother's simpler life. For many of us, the promise of the "happily-ever-after, you-can-have-it-all" future has not been delivered. Instead, we find ourselves confused, unfulfilled, and burnt out.

Many of us scrutinized our mothers and decided that we did not want their subservient, dependent lives. We made a decision to have the financial freedom, autonomy, and adventures that our fathers and other successful men around them enjoyed. As women, we wanted to define ourselves by our own accomplishments.

We thought that in order to achieve success, we had to bury our feminine attributes and exert our alpha male, dynamic, proactive energies. But we were wrong. While it worked, the return was not what we expected. We assumed that we would be able to have a balance of emotional and material rewards, but found that "success" came at great personal cost and sacrifice. By becoming hard-driving alpha females, we gained equality and independence by being the new "better man" at the cost of becoming a better woman.

But it doesn't have to be this way. Instead, we must now learn to move our internal energies away from the masculine world of action, determination, and self-reliance, to reintegrating our own intrinsically feminine forces to attract and receive what we desire. In order to gain control over our lives and discover what makes us truly happy, we need to experience a life shift: to reconnect with our feminine energies of magnetism, receptivity, and intuition.

Life Shift is for everyone who desires to have a life of abundance and fulfillment. By reading this book, you will learn how to transform feelings of failure, frustration, doubt, and loneliness into creative power, opening up new possibilities. As you learn to harness and tap into this manifesting force, you will life shift, becoming not just a dynamic woman who goes after what she wants, but a magnetic female who *attracts* joy, love, and success. A life shift takes your everyday life to the next level, where you can finally get rid of the emotional, mental, and physical obstacles that are holding you back. You will think bigger, live bigger, and realize your dreams. Ultimately, it will bring about a change in your approach that will be dramatic, fundamental, and permanent.

Deep in your heart, you know that you truly deserve to have things come to you without always trying to prove that you are good enough. As women, we know that we are deserving not from a place of ego but from a place in our hearts. My program will help you tap into that place so that you can create your dreams. By engaging your dynamic and magnetic qualities together, without losing or sacrificing one over the other, you can accelerate the process of change and realize that anything is possible. You will have the trust and faith that your dream will happen, as well as the drive and determination to bring it to fruition.

Even with all the obstacles I had overcome, all the things I had accomplished, all the people I had helped over the years, and as prepared as I was, conceiving and giving birth was the greatest challenge

I ever had to face. I can now share my two wonderful children with the world just as I share with you everything I have learned about the extraordinary powers of manifestation. I know that if I could *life shift*, you too will be inspired to live your greatest life. The skills in this book can teach you to create *anything* your heart desires.

My Story

I have two unique perspectives on manifesting life shifts. First, I am a healer. When I was growing up, my initial desire was to help people by changing their emotional states: making them laugh and cry and get in touch with themselves. As a result, I wanted to be an actress because I felt that was the best path for me to reach the most people. Although I was successful, a series of events led me to shift from performing to healing. I became a life coach and emotional healer, first working on myself and then helping my friends, who referred their friends; before I knew it, I had a thriving practice. My business flourished and for the next twenty-five years I found myself traveling all over the world, helping thousands of men and women.

Along the way, I have studied the beliefs, practices, and rituals of Eastern and Western philosophies. I spent time in primitive cultures and investigated the secret teachings of ancient and sacred Egypt, Greece, and China. I learned, practiced, and mastered centuries-old techniques to harmonize the physical, emotional, and mental with the spiritual in a way that balances our dynamic and magnetic energies.

My success with people comes from the fact that they are able to feel the life shift and make dramatic changes quickly, moving into a more positive mind frame and connecting more with their true selves on an emotional and spiritual level. Ultimately, my clients feel happy and start to manifest their dreams and desires. I have seen lives that were examples of frustration, exhaustion, and despair turned around to become rich, fulfilled, and deeply satisfying on all levels: physical, professional, personal, and spiritual.

My clientele often reflects who I am. They are mostly women, and sometimes children or men, who are out there in the world, experiencing the same challenges we all face. Many don't feel the joy and fulfillment that they want; others believe that they are unable to act on their deepest desires. Some are in relationships or marriages that are not working; others haven't been able to find the right person. Some are stressed by their constant need for more money; others are financially successful but are unhappy with their careers. My goal for all of my clients is to bring about a life shift, giving them the tools they need to manifest change in their lives.

The same principles I had used in successfully working with my clients to manifest loving relationships, fulfilling careers, and the financial abundance to fuel their dreams are what led to me being the oldest American woman to give birth to twins. My quest toward pregnancy pushed me to use my alpha energies in a relentless investigation of any physical hurdles that would prevent me from carrying a pregnancy to term. Using both Eastern and Western medicine and a team of healers, I was able to get to the root of my problems and overcome the physical, mental, and emotional blocks that were hindering me. I combined these resources with my ability to use my Magnetic Feminine energy to draw to me what I desired. It is now your turn.

About the Book

No one knows better than I do that getting what you want is hard work, requiring focus, honesty, and faith. My program is nothing less than a road map for transforming your life. The insights and skills described in this book are the result of two decades of research and the successful application of these energy principles in both my own personal transformation and in the lives of thousands of clients. As you put these principals into action and tap into this manifesting force, you will life shift from being an alpha female to becoming a magnetic person who can balance both energies to attract joy, fulfillment, and the love you desire.

In order to awaken the power of the lost Magnetic Feminine, you will follow my journey to many spiritual "power spots." Through these metaphoric adventures, you will acquire the skills to heal and to make your dreams a reality. In the temples of southern India, you will find the secrets of manifestation as you overcome negativity, transforming obstacles into opportunities. In the ruins of Peru's Machu Picchu, you will discover how to connect to your spiritual energy source. In the sacred mystery schools of Egypt, you will learn the secrets of using the power of light.

The journey begins by first determining what it is that you most desire. This is a three-stage process. We start by scratching the surface to identify your most basic wants and needs. Whether they are to lose weight or get a better job or find a companion, these desires need to be fulfilled in order to define your bigger dreams, such as feeling good about yourself, reaping financial success, or starting a family. Through the process of manifesting your dreams, your ultimate destiny and true spiritual self will be revealed.

Every journey requires preparation, and usually some luggage (notice that I didn't say "baggage"). That's where the Life-Shift Tool Kit comes in. These are the techniques that I have been using with my clients for years. They are a collection of tangible, easy-to-follow tools and exercises. These tools will help you get past unproductive thoughts and feelings and keep you on your course. When you use them, you will feel a shift in your energy: You'll reconnect with a deeper part of you and feel revitalized, able to break through any wall of resistance.

Introduction

Once you understand these tools, you can begin utilizing them with a four-part action plan to realize your dreams. The first step is to access your magnetic and dynamic energies. These energies will give you both the strength you need to go after your desires and the ability to attract positive energies and develop the perfect conditions where great things happen.

Next, you will focus on connecting your physical, mental, emotional, and spiritual selves: what I refer to as the Four Bodies. As you strengthen each of these areas, you will rid yourself of physical, emotional, and mental toxins that may be holding you back from success.

The third step is to learn how to overcome the obstacles that may be cluttering your path. In this section you will rid yourself of unproductive beliefs and emotions. Together, we will clear these blocks using your own very powerful spiritual energy. You will be able to move forward in your life, drawing to you what you desire and deserve, experiencing a renewed sense of possibility and positive energy.

The final step is the ability to welcome the support of others into your quest. The alpha female in us finally realizes that we really can't do it all! When you're in your magnetic energy, you're not ashamed to ask for help and support. You feel that we're all here in this life to help one another out. You'll enjoy giving others the opportunity to feel needed. By letting go and opening your heart so that friends, family, or colleagues can help, you are actually moving closer to realizing your dreams.

The second half of the book focuses on attaining specific desires. Each chapter will address unique areas of our lives where we all hope for success, and will show how to manifest these particular desires:

- ✦ Romantic relationships and loving friendships
- ✦ Passion and sexuality

- ✦ Creativity
- ✦ Financial abundance
- ✦ Fabulous career

By following my program, thousands of my clients have been able to manifest all these dreams, and many more. Now it's your turn to point toward your potential, to dream deeply, and to have everything that you deserve.

I have never believed in limiting myself to dreams other people will approve of, or worrying about how you're "supposed" to live your life. I have witnessed too many sad cases of people who have no sense of who they are or what they want out of life, because they have given in to the fear that if they pursue their dreams, they will somehow disappoint everyone and end up alone, living in the land of regrets. I'm here to tell you what I tell my clients who come to me with broken hearts and broken wings, looking for their spirits to be healed: Don't give up on your dreams, no matter how old you are or how many disappointments and obstacles you've had to face. Living in the past and holding on to a fear of the future is no way to live. Instead, by living with and pursuing your dreams, you will find every day fueled with excitement and possibility, and walk the path of your destiny.

LIFE ✧ SHIFT

1

IDENTIFYING YOUR DESIRES, DREAMS, AND DESTINY

1952, Brooklyn, N.Y.

There is a constant theme that runs through my life's desires. When I was growing up in Brooklyn, I loved my family and wanted to please them so much that I was terrified of their disapproval. This fear of being unloved if I wasn't a "good girl" began when I was very young and continued throughout my life. At the same time, my mother raised me to be an independent spirit who was allowed to follow her dreams. This dichotomy led me to focus on achieving dreams that were always about making others happy.

I think that I got my imaginative spirit from my mother: She had always dreamed of being an actress and was a hit in amateur productions at our local church. Because my merchant seaman father was usually gone on one long voyage or another, my mother was left to fill the role of disciplinarian, along with her other familial duties. When my brother, sister, or I misbehaved, Mom would conjure up a bigger-than-life character she called "the Brownie." She would say, "Go hide," and in a loud voice call out, "Oh, Brownie!" This invisible but very awesome presence would immediately respond in an even louder, deeper voice. "Hello, Aleta. This is the Brownie. Have you been a good girl?" Of course I'd always say, "Yes, Brownie." Invariably, the Brownie's voice would respond, "Hm-m-m-m-m . . . that's not what I heard." And in a low, slow voice, he'd say, "I am so sad! I hate to do this, but I am going to have to punish you, Aleta." Then I'd lose a privilege, or my new toy would mysteriously disappear, even if I took great pains to hide it beforehand. Once, the beloved Cracker Jack ring that I was wearing disappeared from my finger as I slept. I could never figure out how the Brownie managed that one!

It didn't take me long to realize that if I followed the rules and did what my mother wanted, I'd be rewarded, but if I didn't, I'd soon suffer the consequences. That's when I began being a "people pleaser." I became the president of my class, head cheerleader, won the National Drama Championships, helped every single person who had a problem, and was the best, most understanding girlfriend in the world to many a needy young man. I would become anxious if someone didn't like me. And no matter how hard I tried, I never felt I had done enough, was good enough, or could trust being loved unless I was doing something for other people.

My mother's dream for me was that I would stay in Brooklyn, live in a neighborhood close to her, marry a lawyer or doctor, and then move the whole family (including her) out to the suburbs. Just as Mother must have felt, my desire to entertain and make people happy led me to dream of the stage. Yet unlike my mother, I chose to follow my dream. While the last thing I wanted to do was hurt my family, I had to gather my courage and leave home to become an actress.

The result was more surprising than I expected. I braced myself for the rejection and disapproval of my family. Instead, much to my mother's credit, she got over me going to drama school in England and ceased pulling her hair out and raving in Italian about her "ungrateful patsa daughter running away from home and doing the nude scene in Hair." Eventually, she threw in her support 200 percent and was my biggest champion. I realized that I deserved the right to pursue my dreams, and I didn't need the approval of others to follow them. Without even knowing it, I had life shifted.

*A*s soon as I started on my own path of realization, I immediately began working with other people. My desire to make others happy continued as I dreamed of becoming a spiritual healer. In my mid-twenties I learned how to heal myself, and then heal others. Again, I followed my heart, did the hard work by using my dynamic and magnetic energies, and was able to manifest this dream. There was a natural connection between my two dreams, which continues today. I use my theatrical talents when I am giving seminars, speaking to the public, appearing on TV, or making videos and CDs to get out my message.

Most recently, I dreamed of becoming a mother. This time, I didn't care what people thought of my decision: I was going to have a baby in my fifties no matter what anyone else said. Again, I was pleasantly surprised. As I went about fulfilling that dream, people were more gracious than I ever could have imagined. People I hardly knew seemed to come out of nowhere with extraordinarily generous baby gifts or offers of time and assistance. My willingness to go after my dream touched others to want to be a part of the magic of seeing a dream come true.

Now I understand my destiny: to teach others to let go of their fears that they will stop being safe, loved, and cherished if they defy other people's wishes. I have learned that people will always come around once you have the courage to identify your desires. Everyone is inspired by other people's bravery. By listening to my heart, doing the work, and following my dreams, I found my destiny.

Desire Creates the Dream that Leads to Your Destiny

Maybe you wish you could lose weight and be healthier and more energetic, or maybe you want to learn photography and take pictures of people and places that fascinate you. Maybe you want to travel, go back to school, or move across the country and start life afresh. You might desire a new job or a new relationship. You might dream of becoming rich or famous, or both. No dream is too small or too big to realize. This book will help you identify what you truly want and help you get it.

The words *desires, dreams,* and *destiny* are not interchangeable. To me, they mean very different things. Anything you can easily identify is probably just the tip of a much larger dream that, together, we will be able to uncover. Those smaller dreams are really your desires: the things or ideas that you want right now. Over time, your desires will create or drive your dream, which then creates your destiny. For example, my desire to make other people happy led me to fulfill many dreams—becoming an actress, a healer, a mother. But my destiny is to teach others what I have learned along the way.

Your journey begins by first identifying your desires, whatever they may be. If those around you can't support your vision or accept your choices, so be it. Your courage may bring up their own deeply hidden feelings of inadequacy and insecurity, but those are *their* issues. More important, don't let their insecurities feed your own. It will take all the courage you have to do this work, so don't let other people's fear reactivate yours. All you need right now is to make the decision to let the fires within identify the inner voice that's urging you on.

Desires

True desire comes from a place deep within that connects you to the voice of your soul. It is an emotional longing that, when fulfilled, urges you to love and be loved. Your desires bring you joy, whether it is a yearning for greater creative expression, romantic love, or the ability to be connected to a group that gives you the feeling of affinity and belonging. You can recognize a desire because when you think of it, you feel contentment and exhilaration. When you are disconnected from it, you feel that you are severed from the essence of your true self.

The energy of desire is the creative force that propels the power of your dreams into the momentum of manifestation and keeps you on the path of fulfilling your destiny. Each of us has the potential to go beyond where we are. Our desires challenge us not to get stuck in the past but to propel ourselves forward, always creating new possibilities and forms of fulfillment for ourselves and others. For example, your desire to be a mother can lead you to find a committed partner, get married, and start a family.

When Karen first came to see me, she was a successful, highly paid advertising executive. As a single mother taking care of her three-year-old twins, Karen couldn't give up her income. She was emotionally torn because she experienced deep feelings of guilt every time she had to leave her children. By the time she came home at night, she was so exhausted from her high-powered, stressful job that she could barely muster up enough energy to play with her children before she put them to bed. Karen knew that these were the important, formative years, and that she was missing a very big part of this precious time having to work to support the family. She felt trapped and frustrated. She came to me crying, "I wish I could stay at home and just be with my kids."

I told Karen that her desire to stay home was the exact emotional energy she needed. At first she became very defensive and began to tell me how impossible that idea was, being a single parent with huge financial responsibilities. I asked her, "What do you love to do above everything?"

"Cooking for my family" was her immediate reply. Karen loved having her family and friends enter her home and feel embraced by the smells of delicious food coming from the kitchen. When she felt particularly stressed, she often kneaded dough and baked magnificent breads and extraordinary desserts to release the tension. She knew that these creative activities brought her back to her center.

I asked her to close her eyes and describe a dream she might have of a happy and fulfilled life in which she could have it all. At first Karen was at a loss; she just couldn't imagine it. I asked her, "If you *could* imagine exactly what you wanted, what would it be?"

It took her a few long, deep breaths, and then all of a sudden she blurted out, "To have a job that I loved doing that would financially support my family so I could stay home and spend more time with my twins. That's what I want!"

I said, "Now close your eyes again and ask yourself if there were no limitations in your mind, how you would imagine yourself making an income around something you really love, like cooking and baking?"

Karen thought for a while and then excitedly said, "I could write a cookbook about the art of home cooking and entertaining. I'd love to inspire women to cook for their families and friends with easy, delicious recipes . . . and maybe start a catering and baking business from my home."

Karen and I worked together for a long time, and finally her dream took form out of her desire. Karen activated her alpha and Magnetic Female energies and began to attract everything she needed into her life. She developed the courage to leave her job, built her catering business, wrote a very successful cookbook, and became a well-known culinary artist sought after by the media. Most important, Karen overcame great odds and manifested her dream of spending quality time with her children.

Accessing Your Desires

Some of your desires may have been clear to you all along. I have always known I was hardwired to entertain others. As a child, I loved to perform for my family and friends, making them laugh with stories I would create and act out. When I was four, I was in the chorus in my cousin Jimmy's children's theater—I remember belting out "Oh, let the sun shine in!" with my whole heart and soul. I graduated to playing Glamour Puss in a murder mystery called *The Nine Girls,* and later, at age twelve, I performed in a summer-stock theater in Plymouth, Massachusetts. I've continued to act, direct, and write throughout my life.

Perhaps you haven't identified your desires or figured out what your dream might be. That's okay. You can start small by getting in touch with one desire and then doing something about it. For example, let's say you love reading to children, and you enjoy watching the smiles on their faces as they listen to your voice. You can volunteer at a local library or give your neighbor a much-needed break by watching her kids. The fact that you took that first small step is enough to begin to ignite your energy, which will ultimately propel you forward to realizing your dreams.

When you live your life to the fullest every day by doing the small things that engage your talents, you make your corner of the world that much brighter, and you remind yourself of what really makes you feel alive.

Revealing Your Desires

Take a relaxed, normal breath in and then exhale. Imagine in your mind's eye that there is a golden sun directly in front of you. Feel its warm rays penetrating your body as you inhale. As you exhale, release any stress, anxiety, or anger that you might be feeling back into the sun and watch each negative emotion burn and disintegrate in the light. As you continue breathing, feel this golden light filling up your heart and ask yourself, "If I could have anything I desire without placing any limitations on it, what would that desire be?" Listen to what your heart begins to tell you. Just allow your desires to come to the surface and make themselves known.

Once you have identified your desires, write them down in a journal or on an index card.

Now that you have recognized your desires, don't talk yourself out of going after what you really want. I promise that you were not meant to have a miserable existence, doing what you hate to do or never really being successful at work or in a relationship. You deserve to be happy. How amazing will your life be once you discover what you excel at or find yourself in a healthy, loving, committed partnership? Until you start going after what you desire, you won't truly be happy, because you are not following the deep longings of your soul.

Positive and Negative Desires

There are often two forces that propel us toward our dreams: I call them positive and negative desires. A *positive desire* is a longing force inside of us that connects us to our higher self, urging us to have greater self-expression and fulfillment. It has a very magnetic quality of connection to it. When you have manifested it, you feel fulfillment because you are satisfying your destiny, your purpose. The following are good indicators that your desires are positive.

Take a look at your journal or index card where you just wrote down your desire. Then ask yourself:

- Does my desire make me feel energized and happy when I think of manifesting it?
- Will fulfilling my dreams challenge me to go beyond where I am, to create greater possibilities in my life?
- Will this desire positively impact me and other people?
- Do I need to call on the help of a higher spiritual source to create it?

If you have answered yes to any of these statements, you are in the *positive desire zone.*

Negative desires come from a void inside of ourselves that we can never fill. These types of desires can come from feeling the hollow spot in your heart because something is missing and no matter how busy you are it keeps nudging you to recognize what it is and to fill the void. The Tibetans refer to this as the realm of the *Hungry Ghost.* No matter how much you feed this ravenous creature, it never feels full or satisfied. It's important to know whether your desires are positive or negative so that you can avoid nurturing the insatiable Hungry Ghost.

The Hungry Ghost

The emotional energies of envy, greed, insecurity, selfishness, fear of not being enough or having enough drive the desires and dreams of the Hungry Ghost. People find themselves in the realm of the Hungry Ghost when they let their insecurities and fears disconnect them from themselves and their core energy. For instance, the feeling that in order for you to have something, you have to take it away from someone else, feeds into your fear, which creates further negative desires.

The Hungry Ghost also represents the addictive side of human nature. Instead of acknowledging and healing feelings of low self-esteem, you might find yourself trying to overcompensate or numb the pain with food, alcohol, drugs, shopping, sex, or any other addictive behavior. These habits offer only momentary relief. Worse, they trick you into continually repeating and augmenting these behaviors, which is why this ghost is never satisfied.

Negative desire can also be generated by one's peers and environment. The parental lingo for this is peer pressure, but even grown-ups can fall victim to this strong desire to be just like everyone else and have what they have. This type of negative desire ultimately comes from a place of discontentment. While it can be a catalyst that allows you to create larger opportunities for yourself and partake in bigger rewards, you will never be able to enjoy your riches until you are able to shift this catalyst into a more positive light.

The following are indicators of *negative desire.* Check these against the desire you just recorded:

+ Are my desires born out of hurt and revenge?
+ Are my desires motivated by proving that I am good enough?
+ Are my desires coming out of a sense of obligation or trying to get someone else's approval?
+ Are my desires coming out of feeling inadequate?
+ Am I envious of what other people have?
+ When I've manifested what I desire, will I still feel unfulfilled?

If you have answered yes to any of these statements you are in the *negative desire zone.*

Unfortunately, negative desires are extremely powerful, and often attractive, at least on the surface. Fear of feeling invisible and not being loved can drive someone to be a great performer, a powerful politician, or a famous sports figure. The fear of being poor has propelled many to become CEOs, barons of Wall Street, and presidents of banks, in positions where they amass great fortunes. But unless desire and longing come from your soul and not the realm of the Hungry Ghost, you will never feel fulfilled and satisfied. What you have accomplished will give you only momentary pleasure and joy until the longing for the next thing begins.

The intention behind the desire is what categorizes it as either positive or negative. Most of us are initially motivated by negative desires because we feel like we have to overcompensate. Somehow, we are not enough. For example, if you recently ended a relationship with someone, you might desire to lose twenty-five pounds and show off by dating some handsome "star" so that your last beau will eat his heart out. Eventually, you'll realize that even though you've lost the physical weight, you're still carrying around the burden of the emotional weight of being hurt by the breakup.

In order to realize your desires and feel good about them, you have to shift negative desires to positive ones. This shift can occur only when you are completely honest with yourself. Honest enough to recognize your negative motives and the hurt they create. Remember, this is not a mind game, it is a shift in the way you manifest your energy. To transform what was once a negative desire into a positive desire, think about the following scenarios. You can still want to lose weight. However, instead of spending your energy thinking about how angry your ex will be because you look so great, use that energy to think about how fabulous you will feel because you love yourself and are happy to be moving on with your life. Instead of going after a particular man who you feel is a trophy that will make others envy you, connect with a deeper desire to find your soul mate, whether it's that man or someone else. Success may be the best revenge, but when you let go of your need to get back at someone who hurt you, you can embrace your desire and create the dream that will truly make you happy.

Release your energy to create your dreams, not to block the dreams of others. Take the step to recognize your negative desire. See it in your hand: a beautiful butterfly ready to take flight. Say to it, "I release you in love and light," and then watch it flutter off. Now your positive energy of desire is available.

Finding Your Deepest Dreams

Your desires are what inspire your dreams. They come to life as you get in touch with and craft your desires into tangible realities. For example, the desire to be free can cause you to dream of having a job that would create financial rewards and structures that allow you to make choices that stimulate your adventurous spirit. The desire not to be beholden to anyone can create a dream of having a life that supports a strong sense of self-reliance and personal power.

Dreams are magical; they emerge from a place of hope and desire deep inside of us. They are the possibilities of life that imprint themselves on the blank canvas of your future. Dreams are messages from your deepest self, whispering to your heart what you were meant to do, to accomplish, and to become. They are catalysts. They give you the platform to regenerate and reinvent your life. No matter what type of challenging circumstance you are faced with, dreams will keep you moving forward.

Many people think that achieving their goals is the same thing as manifesting their dreams. This couldn't be further from the truth! Goals are alpha driven and come from a mental concept: "What do I need to do to accomplish what I want?" Dreams, on the other hand, are magnetically inspired. They need to be created out of our imagination and serve as the bigger picture of what we long to connect to and have in our lives.

Dreams cause you to go beyond your mental and emotional limitations and experiences. They expand your past beliefs about what you feel you can have and deserve to receive. They challenge you to use your own will to succeed, while having the faith and belief in a higher spiritual source that is there to help you manifest what your heart desires. Dreams impart the lesson that all you have to do is ask and hold fast to the intention of what you want to manifest. They challenge you to become single-minded, to not let negative thoughts stop you from doing what is needed to live your dreams.

No matter what passage of life's time march you find yourself in—your twenties, thirties, forties, or fifties and beyond—it is important that you keep your dreams alive! Comedian George Burns had a deep desire to perform, to make people laugh. This dream kept him going well into his nineties. He said, "Age to me means nothing," and "I can't die; I'm booked." He was vitalized by the incredible energy of his desire to express himself, and he was living his dream: to entertain people.

First you have to identify what your dream means to you. Dreams and desires should connect you with your spirit, your deepest yearning to experience love and connection, and to affect the world for the better. So for right now, you may simply want to find the time to run a marathon or play with your kids more often, travel or be a mentor to a young person. If you know there's something that will bring you fulfillment and joy, acknowledge it, go after it, and shape it into a dream that encompasses this as well as your other desires.

It's only natural for our dreams to change over the years, but the deeper dream that drives us toward our destiny remains the same. When I was younger, I recognized that my deepest wish was to touch people on such a profound level that they would be inspired to open their hearts to what they wanted and go for it no matter what. Whatever profession I've had—acting, directing, healing—I have been able to do just that.

Discovering Your Dream

Take out your journal or a pad of paper and pen so that you can fill in the answers to these key questions. They will help you connect the desires you brought up in the last exercise to a bigger dream— a dream that, when you pursue it, will lead you further on your path of destiny.

1. When was the last time you felt genuinely yourself and exactly where you ought to be?
2. What makes your heart start pumping and your creativity kick into gear?
3. What makes you feel younger and more alive than you usually feel?
4. What desires keep coming to the surface no matter how much you try to ignore them?
5. Do you ever feel like you've just plugged in to something big and have an unlimited source of energy? When does this happen?
6. Is there anything you do that is so exciting it makes even the most difficult sacrifices seem insignificant?

Look at your answers and find ways to remind yourself of these dreams throughout the day. Write them on Post-it notes that you stick up around your home. Make a screensaver on your computer that will flash the words before your eyes. Write them on an index card that you can use as a bookmark when you read every night before bed, or put the index card in your pocket or wallet and pull it out several times a day to remind yourself of the dreams you have identified.

For those of you who have lost your faith, I am here to tell you to get back on board; your dreams can come true. For those of you who have never dared to have a dream for yourself because you felt you weren't important enough or felt that your dreams were too big to accomplish, too impossible—forget it! I am a living testament that you can dare to dream. Nothing is impossible when you set your intention on what you want and work with your spiritual energy. That's what I did to manifest my biggest dream, even when people thought I was crazy to want to have children at my age, and as a single parent. We are all put on this earth to live a life of joy and fulfillment by awakening and igniting our true desires and manifesting our dreams. If I could do it, so can you.

When you focus your physical, emotional, mental, and spiritual energies on creating a dream, you set an intention that sends out an energy force into the universe. Your dream and your intention surrounding it are an energy force of creation. It acts as a tuning fork that draws to it what it needs to help it manifest. As if by magic, it creates a magnetic force that draws the circumstances and people to support and give energy to the creation of your dreams. Serendipitous opportunities and events start to occur that you could never have planned.

Celine's Neglected Dream

Celine was someone who had been ignoring her dreams for years. She was a strikingly beautiful woman in her mid-forties, with long, flowing black hair that cascaded down her back and contrasted with her porcelain skin and piercing violet eyes. She came to see me in the hope that I could help her find that special something that would give spark to her life and make her feel enthusiastic again.

Celine looked at me with sadness in her eyes as she told me that she had always wanted to become a professional dancer. As a child, she performed in front of her family every chance she got, imagining that she was on the Broadway stage. However, her mother's disdaining looks made it very apparent that she thought Celine's dreams of becoming a dancer were frivolous. But it was what Celine wanted more than anything in the world, and it broke her heart that her mother didn't approve. Still, Celine wouldn't give up, and when she was sixteen, she landed a job in the chorus line of a Broadway show.

To her deep disappointment, her mother never came to see her perform. After that, she started suffering from anxiety attacks before auditions, and though she forced herself to show up at the calls, she had trouble focusing and became increasingly embarrassed by her inability to do her best. By the time she was twenty-five, she met and fell in love with a wonderful man who asked her to marry him and give up show business. Despite the fact that she was a talented dancer, auditioning had become so anxiety provoking that when she fell in love and had the opportunity to marry, it seemed an easy choice. Celine let go of her dream and hung up her dancing shoes.

After years of being a good wife and traveling companion to her husband, Celine began to feel unfulfilled and restless. Even though she loved her husband, she longed to do something to express herself creatively and define herself separately from her marriage. But she was at a loss as to what that might be.

I intuitively knew that Celine had great dancing ability, even though I had never seen her perform. I suggested that she investigate competitive ballroom dancing, an activity she could enjoy that included her desire to dance and meet new people. Another one of my former clients was an amazing ballroom dancer. She had won the U.S. championship in Latin dance and had opened up her own studio. I knew that she would be a great teacher for Celine, and would inspire her to become a national champion herself.

At first, Celine looked at me as if I had ten heads. "Who goes back into dancing in their mid-forties?"

I said, "You do! You're talented, you've kept in great shape, and I know the perfect dancing coach that you would love. But you have to believe you can do it!"

Celine thought I was crazy at first, but then she decided that maybe I was on to something. She followed my suggestion, started taking lessons with my other client, and reconnected with her love of dancing. After a few months she was up for her first competition, but a week before the event all her insecurities came to the surface and a pestering negative voice said, "You're not going to remember the routine. Everyone is going to laugh at you. What makes you think you can do this at your age?"

She came back to me, anxious, overwhelmed, and feeling like she had made a mistake. I told Celine that dancing in front of other people stirred up a fear her mother had instilled in her all those years ago: that she wasn't good enough to dance in public. It was the same performance anxiety that she had experienced right before she gave up her career to get married. I explained to her that the fears you don't deal with will only come up again and again in other situations until you break through them. I showed Celine how fears create energy blocks, and until she let go of her fear of dancing in front of others, she would never be able to move her internal energy forward so that she could realize her dream of being a great dancer.

Celine decided not to drop out of the competition and began working with me to help her get in touch with her fears and release them so that she could overcome her performance anxiety. As she did this, the competitions became less intimidating for her, and by the end of the year she was winning first-place trophies. Not since she was a child had she felt such deep joy, and it showed in her dancing. No wonder she wowed the judges—she was letting her desire to dance drive her to realize her dream of being a great dancer, and the result was magical. Celine finally claimed who she was and was no longer concerned with her mother's approval, or anyone else's.

Follow Your Heart

Before Celine was able to life shift, she desperately sought her mother's approval to validate her wish to dance. You too may not have been taught to give yourself permission to dream. Maybe you were taught to "be practical," so you programmed yourself to try to achieve the things you thought you were supposed to achieve, and put aside what lit your fire within. You may feel obligated to live out your parents' unfulfilled dreams and pursue society's definition of success, so you go after what you have been told will bring you love, acclaim, and security. Maybe you figure that if you're "good" and become a people pleaser, you'll always be safe, loved, and cherished. But it's not always the case. Regardless of the choices you make, there are unforeseeable circumstances that may alter your path.

We know this from 9/11 and the devastating tsunami in Southeast Asia in 2005. There's no way to tell what the future holds for you. Every once in a while it's a good idea to make a mental checklist of your dreams. Are the choices you are making in your life based on what you truly desire or on what's making you feel safe? Have you let go of certain dreams because you are holding on to disappointments and are afraid of suffering pain again? Are your fears so great that you're distracting yourself from your desires and stopping yourself from dreaming? The only real security is to stay connected to your desires and keep following your dream, creating and living from your full being.

Destiny

One of the biggest conflicts people struggle with is "What is my purpose?" It doesn't matter how successful someone is or how much they have accomplished in their lives. There seems to be an underlying nagging feeling that is urging them on to do something more. I call this search the path to destiny. Destiny is one's life purpose. It is where we are meant to go, the paths we are meant to follow, and the people we are meant to love.

Your desires are the motivating forces that work to help you build and manifest your dreams. Creating and living those dreams place you on your path of destiny. When Dr. Martin Luther King Jr. said, "I have a dream . . ." his *desire* was to free all people from the bondage of oppression. His *dream* was his vision of what the world would look like when he had satisfied that desire: Regardless of race, all people should have equal rights and access to good schools and good jobs, and they should be judged not by the color of their skin but by the content of their character. Because Dr. King went after his dream, he lived out his *destiny*. Pursuing his dream allowed him to keep his eyes on the prize even on the most difficult days.

Destiny doesn't mean that you have no control over, or input in your life and that you can sit back and let things happen because everything is preordained. When you are on your path of destiny, you are participating 100 percent in creating your dreams and living your life's purpose. What is predetermined is your potential, because we are all capable of reaching our destiny. It is your task to expand and grow in consciousness so that you can positively harness your energies to express and experience your destiny path.

On your journey you will find that every step, good or bad, is part of destiny's path. It is our reaction to the obstacles that can derail us. These obstacles you may encounter along the way are expressly there for you to overcome. Some of these "bumps in the road" will actually help to create your destiny. Others are challenges you need to face in order to develop a stronger conviction in your dream.

Many of you may have already realized that your life adventure is not a straight path. You may have started off in business only to switch to something else ten years later. You may have decided to have a family, or retired. Each step of the way is leading you on destiny's path. That is why it is so important not to be judgmental about another's life choices. What may seem reckless and impractical to you may be the very choice that another person needs to make in order to fulfill their ultimate destiny.

Discovering our destiny also helps us evolve and aspire to a higher spiritual self and share our gifts with those around us. When we are following our path of destiny, positive signs from the universe show up at times, seemingly from left field. Money comes through for a project, you turn a corner and meet the person whom you eventually marry. You feel discouraged with the success of a project, and then magically all the pieces and players fall together to help bring it to fruition. These are not merely coincidences; these are forces we have drawn to us through our Magnetic Female energy.

You may be saying, "Aleta, I don't have a destiny. I don't even have a dream. I'm just a regular person." I promise you, we all have a destiny. We all have desires that we can craft into a dream. It's just that most of us aren't taught to give ourselves the chance to think about what we want most. We become afraid and get distracted by what we think we ought to do, and we repress the voice that comes up from our soul. As a result, we can't create our dream and start living our destiny.

Why are *you* here on this earth? What is *your* purpose? If you don't know the answer, start by honoring the desires of your heart because whatever you do that excites you and makes you feel most alive is what will lead you to your destiny. If you really love children, your purpose might be to be a mom or to run a day-care center. If you love to help people, your purpose might be to teach or be a doctor or nurse. If you want to change the world we live in, you might find yourself drawn to doing environmental, political, or social work. I want you to start discovering your destiny now, with this exercise.

Determining Your Destiny

In order to properly complete this exercise, read through the entire exercise once. You may want to have someone else read it to you again while you are performing this visualization. Or you can read the exercise into a tape recorder and replay the tape whenever you are ready.

Take a deep breath in through your mouth. Exhale, breathing out with a sigh. Feel your whole body begin to relax. Inhale, imagining your lungs as a pitcher filling with water from the bottom up, and exhale. Breathe in and out slowly; feel each new breath revitalizing every cell in your body. As you exhale, let go of all worries and tensions. Feel your abdomen expanding as your breath goes deeper, and then exhale. Continue this breathing in an even, relaxed rhythm.

Close your eyes and imagine that you are now facing the Violet Temple of your desires and dreams, a temple that seems to be made entirely of translucent material. The walls and domed ceiling of the temple are luminescent, reflecting a soft violet light. You leave your shoes at the entrance to the temple and feel the moist coolness of its marble floors beneath your feet. As you walk up the steps and enter the temple, you see a violet flame of trust burning in the center of the room. Take a deep breath and allow yourself to be drawn to a place in the room that feels comfortable to you, and sit on a pillow. This is your power spot, your sacred space.

Focus your attention on the violet flame that is in the center of the room. As you gaze into this flame, take your left hand and place it on your heart center, the spot between your breasts. Feel the violet light penetrate this center, giving you a sense of warmth and calm. If you are experiencing any restless feelings, take a deep breath, hold it for a count of five, and then release it as you exhale.

(cont.)

Ask yourself if there are any disappointments, hurts, resentments, and betrayals that you are holding on to. Breathe in and out, letting these feelings come up and reveal themselves as you breathe. Do not try to change them, just let these negative thoughts exist, and speak as if you were talking to the person they are connected to: "I feel sad that you . . ." "I feel angry . . ." Continue until you are really in touch with any dark feelings of disappointment, hurt, sadness, and the resentments of lost dreams. Take a deep breath and hold those feelings for a count of five and then release. Repeat until your negative feelings have dissipated and you feel calmer.

Then take a deep breath, and exhale. Take another deep breath, and exhale. Place your left hand on your heart center. As you breathe in, imagine breathing in a violet ray of light and let it penetrate your heart center. Continue breathing evenly. Focus on your dreams and desires, and then ask yourself the following question: "If I had no limitations on fulfilling my longings and desires, what would I dream of?" Listen to what comes up, and then either take a mental note of it or write it down in your journal.

Place your right hand on your heart center and breathe your dreams into that center. Now think of someone that you love—your child, your beloved, your best friend, or even a favorite pet. Open your mind to this love and receive it without conditions.

Do this until you're feeling a sense of peace and calm. Then ask yourself to free your imagination, and let your answers reveal themselves as you breathe the violet light of trust in and out.

Too many people think that destiny is some huge cosmic prize that goes only to a handful of very special people who change millions of lives during the course of their existence. The truth is that it's not about the numbers of people you affect or the largeness of the legacy you leave behind. What's important is that you get in touch with your unique set of marvelous talents, create your dream, point your feet in the right direction, and begin walking forward. When you do this, you will discover your destiny, and I promise you, it's not an insignificant one. You have a unique purpose in this world.

I know a man who is a brilliant mathematician. He is not a tenured professor at a prestigious university, and he's not a high-paid worker for a large corporation. He drives a bus. Some might say he's an underachiever, but in my book, he is deeply dedicated to his dream. My friend really loves to solve mathematical problems in his head. This desire requires a lot of time spent just sitting and thinking, which he found that he can do throughout the day each time he pulls the bus up to a stoplight. He is content and mellow, able to support his family, and deeply fulfilled. His joy at being able to live his dream touches everyone in his life, from his wife to his kids, from his friends to the strangers who step onto his bus. If that's not success, what is? He's living out his destiny.

Release and Receive

The hardest part of unlocking your dreams is letting go. But that is exactly what you have to do in order to make them happen. Our alpha female nature has adapted to search for security by striving to control any situation, including our dreams. But we must remember that our dreams may be limited by our experiences. Staying in the alpha state of control and remaining attached to a specific plan takes you out of the creative power of the moment and the other options the universe can have in store for you.

Worse, if you can't picture how a dream will manifest, you will assume that it can't happen. Fears and anxieties can block our ability to use our innate energetic powers when we feel that our dreams are impossible and out of reach. You might begin to fear that you don't have the ability or the resources to bring your desires to fruition, leaving you to bury your dreams until you can figure out how they will happen. Meanwhile, you are suffering the emotional consequences of not having what you long for. For example, if your dream is to have a wonderful relationship, get married, and have children, but you just went on yet another really bad date, your anxiety level will start to rise. You may begin to worry that this particular bad date is really an indication that you will be single for the rest of your life. So you might stop dating for a while or subconsciously distance yourself from men who are interested in getting to know you.

True dream manifestation is created by working as though your life depends on the outcome, while maintaining the perspective that you are not in control of the results. Wanting something badly is not enough to make your dreams and desires realities. Neither is going after your dreams with only your alpha energy. In order to really manifest them, you need to set your intentions, feel that you deserve to receive, and let the universe take care of how it is going to happen.

I can guarantee that you will have your big, deep dream, although it may not come in the way you are currently imagining. Whether you are trying to own a house, have a job that you are truly excited about, start your own business, or become an artist, these dreams will most likely take you out of your comfort zone. You need more than ever to align your dynamic and magnetic energies. The key to harnessing these resources is for you to relax, let go, and detach from the outcome.

Think about what happens to your energy when you make a fist and squeeze tight. It gets bottled up and can't flow. When you open your grip, you relax your energy, and it begins to flow, leaving your hand free to touch and receive what comes to you. This is the power of release. When you learn how to harness this power of release, you will no longer feel that you have to force solutions and brandish your will to make things happen. You will see that out of chaos, clarity will come, and you will be led to the channels you need to manifest your dreams.

When you use the power of release, you step into the unknown, which I know can be very frightening. But remember, you are not alone. When we detach from controlling the outcome, we are practicing *divine indifference.* Divine indifference frees up our energy and allows us to create from the idea of uncertainty, trusting that things will ultimately work out for the best. When you let go of your preconceived plan, you open up your most spiritual self to help you manifest out of the realm of possibility.

So much of my work rests on teaching my clients the power of release. To release your desires and dreams, you need to have your focus and intention on what you want to create. Start by getting in touch with your desire and then send out the energy and see how it manifests. For example, I wanted to have children, and I thought the way to go about fulfilling that dream was to fall in love, get married, and have babies. That didn't happen. Instead, I had to switch my intention to think of alternative ways for me to make the dream come alive. Because I let go of the control of how it was to happen, I was ultimately blessed with my two beautiful babies.

Release the Day

It's important to release the tensions, worries, resentments, and disappointments that can pile up during the day, and focus your energy on what you feel grateful for, even if the only good thing you can see is that the day is over. When you release the day, you will create a place of inner peace and calm that allows you to rest and use your energy during the night to rejuvenate, recharge, and begin to align yourself with positive manifesting energy.

When you are in bed and ready to turn off the lights, take three deep breaths, or breathe until you feel relaxed. Then begin to think about the things that might have upset you during the day, including any resentments, worries, fears, or insecurities about your future. Let them come up as you breathe, and exhale them out of your body. Visualize an open window, and as you exhale, release each of your negative feelings out the window and watch them drift away. When you are done, say to yourself, "I let go and release my day. Today was just a short-term situation. Tomorrow will be better." Continue repeating this phrase until you feel that you are in a calmer and more peaceful place. Notice how your body begins to relax. Letting go opens us up to listen and receive the counsel of our inner voice: our higher spiritual self.

It is important to absorb the positive things that happen daily, and store their energy in your reserves. Take a deep breath and exhale. As you inhale again, acknowledge what you felt went well during the day and hold in that breath with a sense of gratitude and accomplishment, letting the feeling of it absorb and vibrate throughout your body. Release your breath, and say, "Thank you for the beautiful moments that happened today. I'm grateful for the joy and happiness I received and for everything I have accomplished."

2

LIFE-SHIFT TOOL KIT

1982, New York City

One of the challenges of being a healer is not absorbing other people's negative energy. I was taught various techniques: washing my hands after each session, burning incense between sessions to clear the room of negative energy, and visualizing myself being protected in a bubble of white light. I practiced all of these with little success: I kept finding myself feeling terribly fatigued and drained. At one point I was unable to rally, and I prayed to God, the universe, to whomever and whatever else was out there, "If you want me to do healing work, you'd better help me figure this out!"

My prayers were answered a few days later, when I was having a massage with a very well-known massage therapist and Reiki healer. His work was completely different from anything else I had felt. He was able to smooth out the tightest knots without causing me any pain, and my tension just seemed to melt away. I asked him what he was doing that made this massage so effortless, and he gave me a knowing smile, like I had uncovered some hidden secret. He told me that he was projecting different colors of light onto my body where it was holding tension. I was eager to learn more, so he directed me to a place called the Actualism Center in Manhattan.

For the next eight years, I discovered the intricate skills of using light frequencies to transform my life and those of my clients. I learned that colors have vibrational rates that work to heal and transform negative energy blocks. Working with color became one of my hallmarks: a most important tool in my metaphorical tool kit.

*M*y healing work can be summed up in a few simple words: *energy transformation.* My clients always think that they have come to see me to fix a specific problem. They may be lonely; hate their job; feel stuck, trapped, or physically ill. But these are really symptoms of a larger, deeper issue. These people are unhappy or un-fulfilled. After the first session, they quickly learn that just being with me isn't going to fix their problems or change their lives. In-stead, I work with them to change themselves. I focus on life shifting their negative thought patterns and actions to a more positive direc-tion, and help them see that there is always a path away from de-structive behaviors and thoughts. Over time, I help them clear the emotional, physical, and mental blocks that are holding them back from living their dreams. When we are successful, their life energy is transformed, and more often than not, they realize that anything is possible. The proof is that they begin to change their lives by mani-festing their dreams.

Through my own personal journey and working with thousands of clients over the past twenty-five years, it has become clear to me that what stops most people from experiencing positive, lasting change is their overall perception about life. The traumas and fears that have affected us over the course of our lives are imprinted in the cells of our body. The body remembers, and when we get upset or are under stress, old feelings of fear and insecurity surface. An internal alarm goes off, and each of our cells begins to vibrate, feeding us back the same dreadful feelings as if they were happening in the present time. That's how we get stuck: by responding to life's challenges with old feelings, beliefs, and, consequently, negative patterns of behavior.

As a healer, I have learned the secrets of how to shift your life at a cellular level. I will help you identify, lift out, and release old negative patterns from your cellular memory. My unique system of using breath, color, power mantras, and focused reflections effectively empowers each cell in your body to create positive, creative energy. This energy creates a new, more powerful imprint, allowing you to use your energy to live a happy and fulfilled life.

The work I do is no "quick fix," but an accelerated awakening to a natural state of balance that propels people to change and grow on their own. What I do is not magic. It takes effort and concentration, and ultimately needs to become a part of your daily life.

Anyone can achieve a life shift through energy transformation. Together, we will make the journey to discover your deepest dream and fulfill it. You will learn from my own experiences and those of my clients. You will go through the process just as they do, using the same tools I use every day.

In order to begin, you have to become familiar with my energy tools, what I like to refer to as my metaphorical tool kit. I wish it were as easy as handing everyone a ThighMaster, but the tools you'll need to reach your potential will engage your mind and emotions as well as your body. I can promise that the lessons in this book and the tools I use will help you grow mentally and emotionally stronger, allowing you to overcome any obstacle and transform your challenges into energy that you can use to fulfill your dreams.

Throughout the book, you will find exercises and instructions on how and when to use each of these tools. The following will help you understand the "why" behind the "how" of the exercises.

Tool #1: Organic Breathing

You may think that since breathing is an involuntary action, if you are not dead you must be doing it right. As with most everything else, breathing is not necessarily that simple. Breathing is a skill involving primarily the lungs and diaphragm and can be done at various levels of expertise. Just as we all can walk, some can walk better than others. Some are awkward or clumsy, some glide, and some speed walk or run with ease. Each of these "walks" takes skill and produces a different result. So it is with breathing.

Additionally, breathing is the bridge that connects our physical and emotional bodies. (This connection is the key to optimal health. As you read this book, this will become even more clear, but for now let's just concentrate on the skill of breathing.)

Our everyday breathing is basically shallow, barely inhaling and exhaling just enough to keep us alive. We use about one-seventh of our true lung capacity. Negative emotions restrict the breathing even further, limiting the amount of oxygen we can take in. Oxygen is key to transporting nutrients to the cells of the body and creating optimal health. Oxygen is critical to brain function. It is essential that you become aware of your breathing and that you exercise your lungs just as you would exercise any other part of your body.

Organic Breathing is a deliberate approach to harnessing your energy and emotions. The goal is to take long, slow, deep breaths in order to slow down your body and mind and really connect with your physical and emotional self. This long, slow, deliberate breathing can regulate the flow of energy throughout the body and allow you to observe or monitor how you feel about and react to the outside world.

There are five basic Organic Breathing techniques I use in exercises in the book. As you become proficient in these techniques, you will see how to use them in your daily life and at a moment's notice.

I provide instructions for each breathing technique. You need to practice these techniques by setting aside time each day. Choose one technique and master it, then move on to the next. Many of my clients practice in their cars at stoplights, or standing in a grocery store line, or when they are watching television. Any of the breathing exercises can be done either sitting upright or lying down in a comfortable position. In order to gain proficiency, I suggest you begin your practice in a quiet place in your home. This should be a place where you will be able to concentrate and be free of distractions. Keep water and a journal or paper and a pencil nearby to record your experience or make notes for future work.

1. **Belly Breathing.** This type of breath is the gateway to all breathing. It lets you experience all the parts of the body involved with breathing. It introduces you to the full power of the breath for energy, relaxation, and connecting with your emotions. Notice when you take a deep breath that you may raise your chest and shoulders. You are not letting the air enter the body past the lungs. In this breath, you want to think of breathing deep into the belly.

   To begin, you may want to put your hands gently on your stomach to feel the breath coming into the belly. Breathe in and out through your nose. Breathe deeply, filling first the belly—you will feel your stomach rise. As your belly fills, you will feel the chest expand and the shoulders rise slightly. As you exhale, notice the air leaving your shoulders, chest, and lungs. Exhale fully, pushing out all of the air and pulling in your navel toward your spine as you finish.

   Repeat this breathing for several minutes, inhaling fully and exhaling fully. Observe any sensations or reactions you may have. This is a great way to relax or even get to sleep if you have insomnia. As you practice this breathing, you may experience sensations all over your body and feel the impact of increasing the flow of oxygen—you may sense what is meant by "connecting" with the breath.

2. **Connective Breathing.** This technique is used when you need to get in touch with your true feelings. Sometimes these feelings are hiding below the surface and the breath can help us access them. You will need to find a quiet space and concentrate fully on your own sensations.

   Breathe deeply and fully in through your nose. Fill your abdomen, lungs, and chest with air. Exhale from your mouth. Exhale slowly and fully. Continue this breathing for several rounds. If you are blocking anything on an emotional level, these feelings can and should begin to surface. You may feel a tight spot in the body or an area of stress. Breathe into this spot or sensation. Continue breathing and listen to what your body is telling you. Observe the sensations and your reactions. Continue breathing and see where it takes you.

   After you finish breathing, make a few notes of what you experienced. Take a moment to reflect, and return to a calm and relaxed state.

3. **Release Breathing** (sometimes called clearing breath). Release breathing is used to let go of negativity. Begin by breathing in through your nose, filling your chest and abdomen. Exhale fully and slowly. When negative feelings and thoughts begin to surface, focus on them as you are breathing. Take a full, deep breath and hold this breath for a count of five. Connect your breath to the negative feelings. Forcefully exhale through your mouth, while thinking of exhaling the negative thoughts and emotions. Exhale fully and completely, leaving the lungs empty. Focus on the release and the change in feeling as the negativity leaves with the

breath. Continue this technique until you feel that you are clear of the negative emotions and thoughts, and feel that you are in a more neutral, centered space.

4. **Energizing Breathing.** You can use this breathing technique to access the revitalizing energy of your breath. This breath brings fresh oxygen into the body and increases the flow of oxygen-rich blood to all parts of the body. Start by taking a full, deep breath in through your nose. Use your belly and diaphragm to exhale forcefully and quickly through your nose. Repeat the strong exhale twenty times. Eventually, you may be able to work up to fifty or one hundred exhales. Notice how the inhales take care of themselves when you exhale fully and rapidly.

In the exercises throughout the book, I have suggested that you use particular breathing exercises, but feel free to work with the ones that perform best for you.

Tool #2: Focused Reflections

When you close your eyes and imagine you are experiencing something, whether you are seeing a ball of light in front of you or hearing words that speak to your heart, you are actually shifting your energy. I call this technique a Focused Reflection.

Focused Reflections are a series of exercises I have created to help you clear your mind of fear and negativity, so you can then focus your mind on what you want to attract, and receive the success you desire. Each Focused Reflection has three parts: first you visualize your success, then you acknowledge the fact that you deserve it, and then imagine that it has already happened. Your Focused Reflections will create a very strong component in using your energy to manifest your desires and dreams. Your life is a reflection of your energy—when this energy shifts, you will start seeing *life-shift changes* as the result.

Throughout the book, I have shared with you simple Focused Reflections that my clients find very effective and that you can do anytime, anywhere. There are also more complex reflections that will require more of a time commitment. For these more involved exercises, find a quiet, comfortable place where you will be undisturbed and feel at ease. Sit in a position that you find relaxing, and keep your back straight. Be sure to wear loose, nonscratchy clothing. I also find that it is very effective to tape-record yourself reading some of the longer Focused Reflections and play them back so that you can let your voice guide you instead of trying to remember all the steps.

Tool #3: Color Immersion

Color is an age-old universal tool used for healing. Over the years, I have learned that different colors can be used to shift energy. I have studied these theories and have developed a unique and successful way of using color in my practice that I call Color Immersion. I use specific colors along with sacred geometric symbols as powerful healing tools. My clients are amazed at the remarkable results they experience. Using these color visualizations, they begin to experience major life shifts and feel a newfound confidence and ability to manifest what they want and need in their lives. The colors help them to clear toxins and raise vibration rates in their physical, emotional, mental, and spiritual bodies. I discovered that once the four bodies are vibrating at a high spiritual level, miracles begin to manifest.

The History

Using color as a tool for healing and transforming is not a new concept. It dates back to 2500 B.C. in Egypt, when the Temple of Karnak was built. This temple consisted of a series of rooms, each with windows of a different color. When the sun shone through the windows, it would fill each room with a particular color that had unique healing properties, and people would visit the appropriate room for treating whatever was ailing them. If they were trying to overcome fears and insecurities, they would spend time in the blue room; if they wanted to heal feelings of rejection and emotional pain, they spent time in the green room; and so on.

I use the same powerful healing colors the Egyptians used in the healing Temple of Karnak as they relate to your seven energy centers. In the Eastern tradition, it is believed that people have seven energy centers at specific points in their bodies. These centers are called *chakras,* which in ancient Sanskrit means "wheels of light." Each chakra relates to a particular set of psycho-emotional issues and stores our past experiences, beliefs, and emotions related to those issues.

Color Immersion has become the cornerstone of my healing work. It threads through every exercise because it has such an extraordinary ability to shift your energy and, by extension, your life. The following lists the colors and their properties as they relate to your seven energy centers. You can use them interchangeably in the exercises throughout the book.

Colors and Their Transformational Properties

Ruby Red: Your first energy center is at your tailbone, and is represented by the color red. This color releases sexual blocks, opening you up to the power of your sexual energy. If I have clients who have trouble expressing themselves sexually, I use ruby red to help release whatever emotional or mental blocks are causing them to turn off their passion. I have them imagine that they are immersed in light, rooting the ruby red color in their pelvic area. This radiant color also has to do with grounding yourself, and harmonizing and empowering personal relationships.

Vibrant Orange: Your second energy center is located two inches below your belly button. Its color is vibrant orange. This color releases insecurities and fears from early childhood, grounding you with a feeling of security and positive self-esteem. If I have clients who have issues of low self-esteem, I use vibrant orange to help them release whatever emotional or mental blocks are affecting them and shift them to the feelings of self-confidence and self-reliance. Orange is also the color I use to help revitalize and restructure how you live your life.

Luminous Yellow: Your third energy chakra is located in your solar plexus. Its color is luminous yellow. This color helps release feelings of powerlessness and victimization, and awakens and strengthens your personal power. When I have clients who feel that they are powerless about changing their lives and are victims of circumstance, I use this color to help them disengage from these negative feelings and strengthen their feelings of personal power and unlimited possibility. This color is also connected to manifestation: When you want something really powerful to happen, you wrap your intention in luminous yellow.

Emerald Green: Your fourth energy center is located in the center of your breasts, and it is represented by deep emerald green. This color helps to release rejection and feelings of loneliness and separation, opening you up to a sense of self-love and deserving. When I work with clients who have just gone through a breakup and feel abandoned, unappreciated, and unlovable, I use this color to help them release these deep feelings and connect with feelings of self-love and personal magnificence. This deep emerald color is also used to attract, heal, and empower your personal relationships.

Turquoise: Your fifth energy center is located at the base of your throat and is represented by the color turquoise. This color helps you to release blocks you may be having in communicating. When I work with clients who are having difficulties asking for what they need or communicating how they feel, I use this color to help them release their feelings and empower them to feel entitlement and abundance. Turquoise also deals with creative self-expression.

Glittering Indigo: Your sixth energy center is located in the center of your forehead. Its color is glittering indigo. This color helps you get in touch with your intuition and connects you to the inner voice of your soul. When my clients don't trust their intuition, I use indigo to help them release their fears so that they can follow their inner voice. Using this color strengthens their faith and trust in their inner knowing and guidance. Glittering indigo also helps bring a higher spiritual perspective to negative situations and experiences.

Translucent White: Your last chakra is located six inches above your head, and is represented by translucent white, which reflects your higher spiritual self. When I work with clients who are feeling hopeless and have a difficult time feeling the support and love of a higher power, I use translucent white to help release the feelings of despair and fear of the future, as well as strengthen their connection to a force that is greater than themselves. Translucent white is also connected to the power of manifestation.

There are other important colors not related to your energy centers that you will find in various exercises throughout the book. *Hot Pink* releases criticisms and self-condemnation, opening you up to feelings of gratitude and unconditional love for yourself and others. *Cobalt Blue* cuts through fear and gets to the truth, opening you up to faith and belief. *Purple* releases limitation and scarcity, opening you up to abundance and joy. *Silver* releases guilt and addictions, opening up your magnetic ability to receive. It relates to the highest aspects of feminine nurturing, receptivity, and intuition. *Gold* transforms negative energy into the positive, creative energy of possibility. It embodies the most positive attributes of the male energies, including protection, action, and persistence.

Visualizing Color

In the Focused Reflections throughout the book, I will ask you to visualize a particular color. If you are having a hard time visualizing, don't worry; not everyone can easily see color. You can use your imagination to bring it to your mind's eye by thinking of something that represents the color. For example, if the color is gold, think of a handful of gold coins or a gold bracelet. Some of you might actually feel what the color looks like, the way a blind person would. The more you surround and immerse yourself in the colors, the easier it will be to release the blocks to manifesting your dreams. Your environment will constantly be a support as you are vibrating at a level of manifestation (the level where miracles happen).

Color Support Tools

While you practice, you may also want to find a small token or crystal in each of these colors and hold on to it while you are doing the exercises. You can buy sets of colored eyeglasses, which enable you to "see" the world in different colors. Or, if you like, dress in a particular color to influence your mood. Change the color of your environment by painting the rooms you spend a lot of time in, or accent your space with blankets, pillows, and objects within a certain color spectrum.

One fun exercise that my clients say really makes a difference in how they experience their daily life is to randomly select a color that will support a positive outcome. Each morning, open this book to the pages where the colors are listed and close your eyes. Ask yourself, "How do I want to live my day?" Then ask yourself, "What color do I need to support that outcome?" Dangle your finger over the list of colors. Let your finger rest on a spot and read the color that you need to work with. As your day progresses, remember to see yourself doing everything you want effortlessly as you surround yourself with that color.

Tool #4: Energy Baths

My work is all about detoxification, eliminating pollutants that are blocking physical, emotional, or mental energies. All the tools in the tool kit support this detoxification in different ways. Organic Breathing keeps energy moving. Color Immersions help release and transform dense negative energy, raising it to the higher, faster vibration rate, connecting to the spiritual self. Energy Baths help release physical, emotional, and mental toxins through the vibration of the water.

If you think baths are just about getting clean, you're missing out on the benefits of one of my favorite Life-Shift Tools. In ancient times, baths were used to soothe, relax, and heal. You can turn your bathroom into an energy spa by feeding your senses with delicious aromas, sensuous oils, soothing music, and soft, dim lights. Nurturing yourself is key to experiencing the magnificent energy of your

Magnetic Feminine. One of my clients enjoyed her Energy Baths so much that she finally put her shower curtain away for good!

Each of the baths listed in the book requires the use of special ingredients, such as aromatic oils. Each oil has a specific property and color used to release your blocked energy. For example, the essential oils of jasmine, rose, lavender, and chamomile will stimulate your brain centers to promote relaxation and a sense of release and healing. If you need to get in touch with your alpha energy, take an energizing bath of peppermint, rosemary, or fennel. Alternatively, you can take a soothing bath with the oils of neroli, bergamot, or juniper to awaken your magnetic energy. Though not an essential oil, Epsom salts can ground you, put you in touch with your creative energy, add needed magnesium back into your body, and help rid the body of physical toxins.

For any bath, set aside a time when you know that the background noise will be minimal, and create a sensory experience that takes you out of your head and into your body and emotions. The baths in this book require a minimum of ten minutes; a longer twenty-minute bath is even better for shifting your energy and, as a bonus, rehydrating your skin.

Basic Detox Bath

Fill your tub half full of warm water. As you enter, adjust the temperature so that it feels comfortably hot. Pour in one cup of apple cider vinegar and two cups of sea salt or kosher salt as the bath continues to fill, and add a bit of liquid soap or shampoo to start the bubbles going. When the tub is full, immerse your body up to your neck.

Take a deep breath in and exhale. Imagine a golden sun six inches above your head, and as you begin to inhale, feel its warm rays penetrating your body, pouring into every cell. As you exhale, feel as if you are releasing tensions and any negative feelings you may have.

Repeat the breathing until you have gained a sense of peace and calm. This releasing bath can get your Magnetic Feminine ready to receive the good things around you. When you are done, pull the plug and watch the negative energies go down the drain. If you are feeling especially negative that day, it's a good idea to complete the bath with a shower, exfoliating any excess negativity that might be clinging to you.

Tool #5: Power Mantras

Your words and thoughts have power. Mantras have been an integral part of Eastern religious practices for centuries. They are used to create spiritual evolution by purifying, healing, and breaking negative patterns. Hindus believe that saying the sacred syllable "Om," which is part of many mantras, actually connects you to the Divine. The more these ancient mantras are repeated by different people, the more power they have.

I have created the Power Mantras to help you quickly access your positive energy by declaring to the universe who you are and what you desire to manifest. Like color does, your thoughts and the words that you speak have a vibrational rate that can put you in or out of alignment with the vibrational rate of your desires and dreams. Power Mantras will put you in harmony with the vibrational rate of what you want, which can help you attract the situations, financial resources, and people that you need to manifest what you long for.

Power Mantras are dynamic as well as magnetic tools that can activate your emotions as well as imprint your mind with positive messages. My Power Mantras use practical, everyday language. Their language will actually change the energy inside and around you from negative to positive, allowing you to attract positive people and situations. They make you feel good about yourself and the possibilities of what you want to create.

Throughout the book, I've written specific Power Mantras for different situations. Here are some of the Power Mantras that my clients say help them to rapidly shift their beliefs from negative to positive:

- ✦ Shift defeat to expectations of success: "I am creative resilience."
- ✦ Shift fear to an expectation of power: "I am indomitable courage."
- ✦ Shift self-doubt to an expectation of higher support: "I deserve to receive."
- ✦ Shift hopelessness to optimism: "It hasn't happened *yet.*"

Designing Your Own Power Mantra

You can also create your own Power Mantra. If you want to do this, consider the essence of what it is you want, and boil it down to one statement. Here are some tips for writing your own effective Power Mantra:

1. **Keep it simple.** Say "Positive people are coming into my life now" instead of "I am happy because I am now attracting more positive people into my life that can love and support me and remind me of what I really value."
2. **Keep it positive.** Say "I am attracting a man who loves, adores, and appreciates me," instead of "I won't attract any more jerks."
3. **Keep it in the now.** Your Power Mantra should be in the present tense, as if it were already happening. Say "I am attracting supportive friends" instead of "I will attract supportive friends" or "I want to attract supportive friends." If you can't see what the difference is, try saying "I want joy in

my life" or "I will have joy in my life" and feel how much weaker an emotional response you have than if you say the more forceful "I am experiencing joy."

4. **Speak your truth.** If you don't feel comfortable asserting that something is already happening, use the words "I'm in the process." If you just ate three huge bowls of pasta, it may feel dishonest to tell yourself, "I have willpower"; instead, say "I'm in the process of developing willpower." The more real the Power Mantra is for you, the more effective it will be.

Power Mantras do not have to be spoken out loud. I have one client who recorded her personal Power Mantras and plays them in the car when she's driving the kids to school, or whenever she feels like she's getting into a negative space. Another client writes her Power Mantras on Post-it notes and places them in various locations around her home—on the refrigerator, the computer, the telephone, or on her bathroom mirror.

Tool #6: Power Prayers

I find that prayer is a very integral part of my Life Shift program. It immediately puts you in touch with a power greater than yourself that is there to support you and help you create whatever it is that you desire. Prayers are appropriate when you want to ask the divine energy to help other people heal or manifest perfect abundance. I have my clients use them when they need divine assistance in financially challenging situations, with health issues that need resolution, and in times of work- or personal-relationship crises.

There are many different types of prayers and blessings, and you can effectively use them not only to connect with your higher power but also to change your life and achieve your desires and dreams. Prayer is a direct pipeline to your spiritual body. It can quickly shift you out of the feelings of powerlessness and insecurity into feelings uplifted by the energy of joy, peace, and calm.

Many of us grew up thinking that prayer is something you do only when there is a crisis. We start making contracts with God, like "I promise I'll do this if you give me that," or "God, if you just give me this one thing, I will never ask you for anything else again." Then, when the next crisis or strong desire comes along, we try to renegotiate our deal. When we think of prayers only as poker chips to use in the game of life, we overlook their incredible capacity for helping us shift our lives.

Like many people, I always thought that the more worthless you felt when you prayed to God, the faster God would help you out. Being a Type A personality, I dove right into being humble. There I was as a child, at six o'clock mass every morning, on my knees, pounding my chest, saying, "Through my fault, through my fault, through my most grievous fault." After I felt that I had sufficiently placated God with my worthlessness, I immediately launched into my list of what I wanted God to help me or my family and friends with. Sometimes it worked, and sometimes it didn't, in which case I'd just beat my chest more.

It wasn't till years later, at a Unity Church service with Eric Butterworth, a well-known Unity minister, that I heard that the more effective way to pray is to come from a place of deserving and gratitude—as though you have already received what you are asking for. I tried it and found that God answered me a lot faster, not necessarily in the way I'd planned but always with a positive outcome. Now I know that when you ask God for help, it's best to keep it simple and from the heart, and frame your prayer as if it is already answered—and remember to express thankfulness.

If you don't have traditional prayers that you feel help you connect to a higher being, my Power Prayers are simple prayers you can use to connect with your spiritual body. Power Prayers help you directly resource the energy of God. It is kind of like you are having a communion, a two-way conversation with an energy source. Unlike Focused Reflections, you are not visualizing an outcome. Instead, you are connecting to an energy source that is supporting your creation. The following is a sample of a Power Prayer. There are many more scattered throughout the book.

Thank-You Prayers

These are great prayers when you are feeling overwhelmed by how much you have and handle, or if you feel as if your cup is half empty, not half full.

* Thank you for this gift of life. Help me bring joy to myself and others this day.
* Thank you for this wonderful meal that I am sharing with my loved ones today.
* Thank you for the amazing people you have brought into my life. Keep them coming.
* Thank you for being there. I really need a miracle. Surprise me.

By using any of these tools to release negativity, you will connect with the Magnetic Feminine and alpha energies, allowing you to begin an energy transformation. By using all of the tools you will learn how to life shift. You will be able to manifest your dream and replace feelings of fear with joy and vitality.

Now that you have the tools, you can follow my journey as I take you through the five-step process of manifestation:

1. Determining what it is that you really want: desires, dreams.
2. Identifying your obstacles: What's still holding you back?

3. Connecting the four bodies: ridding yourself of emotional, mental, and physical toxins as you connect with your spiritual body.
4. Harnessing both your magnetic and your dynamic energies: matching action with attraction.
5. Receiving support: opening yourself to the help of others.

Let your journey begin. . . .

3

STEP ONE: ACCESSING YOUR MAGNETIC AND DYNAMIC ENERGIES

Summer of 1968, Amsterdam

The three cups of black coffee, the French cigarettes, and the half a diet pill I had to have every morning were no longer working their magic. I lay motionless on the bed, and when the phone rang, I didn't have the energy to answer it. I summoned up what felt like the last bit of strength I would ever have and heaved the receiver up to my ear. A hoarse and gravelly hello *was all I could manage in response to my very concerned and dear friend, who asked, "Are you okay?"*

For the first time in my life I said, "No. Something is wrong. I can barely move."

I knew I was in trouble. I had worn myself out trying to be everything to everyone: to be loved, appreciated, and successful in my career as an actress. I was performing in ten shows a week, rehearsing another show on the side, never turning down personal appearances, and taking dance and singing lessons. For days at a time, I lived on a model's diet of whipped egg whites seasoned with a teaspoon of honey, followed by a bowl of lettuce (no dressing, yum!). Whenever I started to get hungry or the inevitable fatigue began to overcome me, I'd just pop another diet pill, pour another cup of coffee, or light up a cigarette. Yet on that day, my body just refused to go along with this insane program and simply shut down.

The buzzer sounded. After what seemed like an eternity, I dragged myself to the door and opened it. My friend took one look at me and immediately said, "Get dressed. We're going to the hospital."

When we arrived at the hospital, they put me in a bed, took my temperature, and drew out a couple syringes of blood. The doctor said he wanted to do some quick tests, and when he came back, his face looked grim. "I'm afraid I'll have to keep you here until further notice," he reported.

"Are you kidding?" I said with a note of panic in my voice. "I've got a performance tonight! I can't possibly stay here!"

"I'm sorry," he said, "but you have infectious mononucleosis. You're not going anywhere."

I was stunned. My mind simply couldn't compute this information. The doctor asked me if I had any friends or family who could take care of me. Of course I did, but everyone I knew was on another continent and what seemed like a whole other world: back in Canarsie, Brooklyn.

In a quiet voice, I asked the doctor, "How long till I get back on my feet?"

"No less than a year," he said.

A year?! This couldn't be. I was twenty-two and I had the lead in Hair. I was negotiating with a Dutch record producer about cutting my own album. Just two days before, I had been offered a leading role in a Dutch television movie about Salvador Dali. Things were really starting to break for me after years of hard work. I had my life all planned out: By the time I was twenty-five, I expected to have a fabulous career as an actress, be married, and have a child. There was no doubt in my mind that I could make it happen, because I was young, talented, and invincible. I was going to do it by sheer force of will. And now I was going to have to go back to Brooklyn. God couldn't be that cruel!

But the doctor insisted that for the next year I was to stay home and do nothing. My mother would have to take care of me.

"Is this it? Is my life over?" I wondered. I just couldn't figure out why

things weren't happening as I had planned. I had worked hard, doing everything I thought I was supposed to do. And yet that morning I had slammed into the wall, exhausted and ill. Why did things appear to be going my way, only to be dashed at the last minute? Was I losing faith in my dreams?

Defeated, I went back to Brooklyn to recuperate. For months I lay in bed, depressed. Finally, not knowing where else to turn, I dropped to my knees and prayed to God for help. As fate would have it, a few days later I had a visit from a childhood sweetheart who stopped by to see my mother. He gallantly suggested that I visit his acupuncturist, who might be able to speed up my recovery. At that point, I was ready to try anything.

The next week, my former beau dropped me off in front of a run-down tenement in Chinatown. As I climbed the steps, trying to catch my breath, I somehow sensed that whoever was on the other side of the door would have some answers for me. A bell with a little red tassel hung next to a drab-looking door. I pulled on it, and before I knew it, an energetic, spritelike woman was peering up at me. "Madame Woo?" I tentatively asked. She nodded.

Her kind, wise eyes gave me permission to pour out my tale of woe. I will never know if she understood a word of what I was saying, but after I had shed my last tear, she lovingly took my right wrist and put her fingers on my pulse, then took my other wrist and did the same. After a few moments, she smiled, saying, "I fix." Ushering me into her treatment stall, she stuck hair-thin acupuncture needles into me, saying something about "balancing my energies." I had no idea what she was talking about, but within a month, my strength came back in full and I quickly packed my bags, kissed my mother good-bye, and headed out of Brooklyn to seek my fortune in Manhattan.

The hours I spent with Madame Woo made a profound difference in my life. Not only did she help me get physically well, she also imparted to me the ancient Chinese secrets of how to attain emotional well-being by balancing my energies. What I learned became a cornerstone of my work as a healer and a very important factor in my pregnancy. It's what has allowed me to reach my own desires, dreams, and fulfill my destiny as well as help my clients manifest their own.

Too Much of a Good Thing . . .

I came to realize that the reason I had gotten so very sick was that, like so many people in our "Just do it—now!" culture, I had been running on only my alpha, dynamic energy. I was pushing hard to create my dreams by doing everything I possibly could to make them happen. In so doing, I had been neglecting my feminine magnetic energy. Until now, I'd had no idea that within me was energy that would draw to me what I wanted, allow me to retain what I'd brought in, and let me watch my dreams come true—all without my having to work so hard every minute. But that is exactly what I learned from Madame Woo.

Your Dynamic Energy

I know that many of you are like I was—more comfortable giving than receiving, doing instead of being. When you are constantly chasing your dreams, you feel like you are in control and less likely to be rejected. This go-go-go energy is your alpha or dynamic energy.

Dynamic energy is a critical ingredient in making your dreams come true. It puts the wheels in motion. As Descartes said, "Faith without action is death." Traditionally, dynamic energy has been seen as a male energy. When the men of ancient Rome needed a bridge, they built it, and if they needed to vanquish an enemy, well, as Caesar said, *"Veni, vedi, vici"*—"I came, I saw, I conquered." You just can't get any more straightforward, decisive, and determined than that.

My grandfather understood this energy quite well. In an effort to keep all his daughters and granddaughters on the straight and narrow, he'd say to us, *"Figlia Mia,* my dear daughter, you think a man loves you, but you are the bird and the man is like a hunter who sees the bird in the tree and then shoots it down." That was an interesting warning about the male need to conquer, coming from my very handsome and dapper grandfather, who loved to tell the story of how, as a young man, he whisked my grandmother away from her wealthy father, hiding her from the entire town for days as they lived in a giant wine barrel. I guess Grandpa knew just what he wanted and did what he had to do to get it, and he didn't sweat the consequences.

Many women still tend to go too far into their dynamic energy. We work hard all day at home or work, and then we spend our free time helping others or planning what else we have to do. If you're feeling you've got to do it all and be it all to achieve your dreams—take on all the responsibility, solve the problems of everyone around you, accommodate everyone's needs, and so on—you're probably experiencing Dynamic Burnout, just as I was.

You may find yourself so exhausted and anxious from "doing" and "proving" that you just close down and stop striving to do *anything*. Many of you have grown up feeling that you are not enough, or that your worth is determined by other people's approval. You may feel like you are so overextended that if someone asks you to do one more thing, you are going to explode and shatter. The pressure you are feeling is most likely internally generated by your need to please, an inability to set boundaries, and taking on responsibility for the happiness of others.

Symptoms of Dynamic Burnout
+ You're on edge and stressed out, feeling like you can't do one more thing.
+ You seek comfort in food, TV, alcohol, or shopping.
+ You feel numb, and have no interest in sex or relationships.
+ You are experiencing low energy or sudden health problems.
+ You feel resentful because your life is revolving around other people.

You might keep going full speed ahead even when you're feeling these symptoms because we often convince ourselves that at some point, everyone we're giving to will feel nurtured and healed enough to reciprocate. Unfortunately, people get spoiled by your willingness to be overgenerous and overextended. Instead of asking you what you need or how you're feeling, and taking care of you for a change, they'll probably just keep expecting you to listen to their problems and nurture them. As a result, you end up feeling drained and resentful.

This burnout is not terminal, and you can turn it around by opening up your magnetic energy and allowing *yourself* to receive.

Your Magnetic Energy

The magnificently subtle energy of magnetic attraction has often been represented by the silvery, luminous moon, which tugs at the ever changing tides. It is associated with the creative life force and traditionally has been thought of as a feminine, sensual, attracting energy. Ancient Greek women realized and exalted in the power of this awesome force. Through the miracle of birth, they recognized the power of the Magnetic Female to attract, nurture, and carry to fruition the creation of a child. This magnetic ability is the same energy that we tap into when we *attract* a partner, when we *draw* to us the support necessary to achieve a goal, and when we *receive* and *experience* the love and appreciation we need in our personal as well as our professional relationships.

The pulse of your Magnetic Female is the heightened desire to seduce while surrendering, receive while giving, and ultimately to merge with your alpha dynamic energy. The Magnetic Female energy is an active yet receptive force as it draws to you the things you desire to create in your life. Many of you have experienced this powerful but subtle energy while making love. When you are open and receptive and surrender to the dynamic masculine alpha energy of your partner, you feel a oneness, a merging, a sense of completeness.

The power of the Magnetic Feminine rests in the power to believe that we deserve to receive and that we have personal value. It's the ability to magnetically keep what we manifest, continuing to let it build and grow in our lives.

In the modern era, we tend to dismiss the power of attraction. We scoff at the idea that we can draw in and attract love, appreciation, and support. We think that we have to do it all, and need to convince others to do what we want them to do. We don't trust that we are important or valuable enough to attract their help. You may be saying to yourself, "Aleta, this magnetic energy sounds great, but I've always been a workhorse. I'm the one who's always giving. People aren't going to suddenly start giving to me." Well, you're wrong. You've been doing all the work because you didn't know the secrets of using your magnetic energy, and you're blocking yourself from drawing in support.

For those of you alpha females who are used to achieving your dreams through mere force of will, focus, and "pit bull" determination, it can be hard to trust that if you don't do it all yourself it will get done or that if you ask for help it will be there. Especially if you are faced with the challenges of recovering from a breakup, change of careers, or financial or health challenges, your natural inclination is to use your alpha energy to start pushing for what you need "to do" in order to overcome. But don't do it. Try to harness your magnetic energy by opening yourself to support. When you use your magnetic energy, you'll get much more accomplished because other people will be drawn to you to help you out. Instead of feeling burnt out, you'll feel loved and valuable: an appreciated member of the team.

The Differences Between Magnetic and Dynamic Energies

Let's go over some of the major differences between alpha and magnetic energies. This way, you'll see why it is so important to learn how to harness your innate ability to get what you want out of life.

Going for It vs. Drawing It to Us

Your dynamic alpha energy puts your desires and dreams into motion through focus, action, persistence, and determination. In the world of the alpha, the elation of checking items off an extensive "to-do" list is the adrenaline rush that creates feelings of adulation, self-value, and accomplishment. Whether you are in the business or creative worlds, a mother running a household, or both, the belief is that if you go after what you want, you will get it.

Your Magnetic Female works as a force that attracts what you desire through the subtle energies of softness, receptivity, creativity, and intuition. It is the dreamer within us, our creative imagination that taps into our desires and helps us build our dreams. The famous seductresses in history knew the magic of "allure." For example, Cleopatra scented her body with the sensual-smelling oil of jasmine to seduce Antony. She actively drew him in by applying this passionately stimulating oil to her body, letting its compelling fragrance and her exotic beauty reel him in.

Results vs. Patience

When you are in your alpha energy, you want results now. If you planted seeds in the ground and they are not sprouting fast enough, it's time to toss those aside and plant new seeds.

In the world of the Magnetic Feminine, "patience pays"—it allows things to take their course and unfold. When you are in your Magnetic Feminine, you relax into the flow and timing of things and do not push for the results. Like a maker of fine wine, you let the grapes reach their peak before you pick them.

Unfortunately, we've gotten used to fast-food drive-throughs, sitcoms where any problem can be solved in just half an hour, and promises of six-pack abs in just ten minutes. Surely, patience takes too much time! If you find yourself getting caught up in the "hurry up" mentality, this exercise will help you stretch your patience muscle.

Patience Pays

Whenever you sit down to eat a snack or a meal, take a deep breath and exhale. Breathe in and exhale again, and see yourself and your food surrounded by the glow of soft lavender, the color of patience. Sit with this awareness of the lavender light for a few moments. Feel it enveloping you.

Then, as you take your first bite, chew it twice as long as you normally would. As you chew, pay close attention to the taste of the food and its texture as it touches your tongue. Feel the movement of your jaw and your tongue. Do this for each bite of food until you are finished, no matter how long it takes.

You can use this exercise to savor other everyday experiences as well—folding laundry, helping your children brush their teeth, driving to work, and so forth. Slowing down your life and paying attention to the task at hand instead of charging forward toward your goal will help you develop your ability to be patient.

Self-Reliance vs. Working Together

Alpha energy is about self-reliance and coming up with the answers on your own. When you are in your alpha energy, you will feel responsible for coming up with the answers: Asking for help or consulting others would be considered weak.

When you are communicating with others and working together to figure out a solution, you are using your Magnetic Female Energy. This allows you to be comfortable listening to and responding to the needs of others and working with them. If there is a problem, the magnetic energy seeks out the solution through interaction and communication with other people.

Shelly, a client of mine, is a very successful CEO of an apparel company. She uses her Magnetic Female to consistently reach her sales goals by working with the buyers, being flexible, finding out what they need, and finding solutions. Together, Shelly and the buyers make things work.

The next time you get frustrated, try to elicit cooperation from other people, or try this quick exercise.

Connection Leads to Cooperation

The goal of the reflection is to try to energetically connect with another person.

Use your Belly Breathing until you are completely at ease. Then imagine yourself sitting directly opposite from this person. Imagine a pink orb hovering six inches above your head. Feel the downpour of energy as you breathe in. As you breathe out, feel that you are releasing any anger or resentments you may be having about this situation or person. Send out pink light from your heart center directly into theirs, and feel the pink energy coming back. In your mind, ask the person what they need from you in order to resolve the situation, and see if you can give it to them. Then tell them what you need from them and see if you can feel the energy coming back to you. If they can't give you what you need, ask them why, and take in that information. Last, imagine a positive outcome for the situation and surround that with hot pink light. Release it by saying aloud, "And so it is."

Hard Facts vs. Intuition

An alpha decision is a very practical and fact-based approach. When you are in your alpha energy, you make decisions based on tangible facts. If a hospital had a greater success rate at healing cancer, you would choose that hospital rather than choosing a doctor you had a good "feeling" about.

When you are in your Magnetic Female Energy, you make decisions based on gut feelings. Somehow, you just know you are right, and you honor that. You are using your sixth sense, an inner voice that gives you information and directs you to make choices. You may have a feeling that you should go down a certain street, and when you follow your instinct, you end up meeting someone whom you wanted to see, whom you haven't seen in years, or who could possibly change your life.

My client Emily was walking down the street on a freezing cold winter day and decided she had to pop into a store to warm up. She ducked into a little antique shop that she had always thought looked interesting, started chatting with the owner, and got a very powerful feeling that she needed this person in her life. The urge to reconnect with him was so strong that she went back to the shop on another day, determined to start up a conversation and get to know him better. Six months later, Emily and the antique store owner were engaged, and they've been happily married for years.

Despite all the evidence that gut instincts can be good ones, many people in our culture dismiss and even ridicule these hidden ways of knowing, whether they are sensing "vibes" or listening to "feminine intuition." No wonder so many of us tend to dismiss our intuition as a trick of the imagination. The following exercise will get you in touch with your intuition.

What Your Gut Knows

Set your phone to ring at least four times before going to tape or voice mail. The next time it rings, take a deep breath, close your eyes, and visualize yourself holding the receiver, surrounded by a blanket of purplish-blue light. Ask yourself who is calling. After you've taken this short moment, answer the phone and/or look at your caller ID. Were your instincts right?

Do this every time the phone rings for several days. One of my clients was surprised that after a week of doing this, she would find herself thinking, "Wow, my cousin Laura is calling? She never calls at this time of night," and sure enough, when she picked up the phone, that's who was on the other end.

Magnetic Energy Increases Flexibility and Creativity

When you tap into your magnetic energy, you open yourself up to all sorts of possibilities. You can dream up solutions to your problems, regroup, and figure out a new approach. Look at Cher and Madonna, two women who are continually finding new ways to express themselves. But so often in our culture, the message is "Do it the way we've always done it." When I helped my brother, Curtis, form the Guardian Angels twenty-seven years ago, the media and the police all said we couldn't possibly create an effective neighborhood watch program, because no one had ever done what we were trying to do. Today, the Guardian Angels have chapters all over the world, and New York City's notoriously crime-ridden areas of Times Square and the theater district that the Angels began patrolling are safe, teeming with tourists and flourishing businesses.

Magnetic Energy Doesn't Mean Doing Nothing

Magnetic energy is integral to the creation of your deep dream. But just like with dynamic burnout, you can't rely on magnetic energy to do all the work for you. There are some women who spend too much time waiting and not enough time doing. When you dismiss the importance of your dynamic force, your life can become stagnant. This is what one of my clients, Fern, learned.

When I first met Fern, she was a vibrant young comedienne in her thirties, but she lamented to me that her career was going nowhere. She couldn't yet make a living in comedy, so she worked at restaurants and found this very frustrating. "I've paid my dues!" she said. "I've waited forever to be famous!" Everyone thought she was talented and funny: Even a psychic had told her she was going to have a sitcom by the end of the year and would be able to burn that waitress apron. Fern believed this was true, and she felt entitled to the success she had coming to her. But when I asked her some direct questions about her career, it was clear that she wasn't actively pursuing it: She hadn't performed at nightclubs (even on newcomer nights), auditioned, or tried to get an agent.

What Fern needed was to use her dynamic energy to become proactive and her magnetic energy to attract opportunities and the jobs she wanted. I urged her to stop using her long hours at the restaurant as an excuse and make the time to do three things each week toward achieving her goal. It took her a while to get over her discomfort about getting out there and doing what she needed to do, but I had her visualize her desires surrounded with golden light, and before long, opportunities started opening up for her. She pounded the pavement and made the calls to agents until she got a good one, eventually moved to Los Angeles, where most sitcoms are cast and filmed, and started to audition for comedic roles. She used the power of her Magnetic Feminine in her Focused Reflections to envision the jobs that would come to her. Every day she would try to be actively patient so that she wasn't as anxious as before. While she hasn't gotten her sitcom yet, she's making a living as a comedienne. She finally feels like she is on destiny's path, doing what she was meant to do, and she is thrilled about it.

Fern came to realize that when you're in your dynamic energy, you feel like you can conquer the world and make your dreams and desires come to fruition. Draw on your dynamic energy, as it will in turn support your magnetic attraction. It is the relationship of these two forces—the alpha doing and the magnetic receiving—that is the key to the power of manifestation.

The Engagement of Your Dynamic and Magnetic Energies

One type of energy is not better than the other; they each have their place and are very important in the dance of life. You need your dynamic energy to actively take charge and put into motion what you need and want. You need your magnetic energy to draw to you the things you desire. Your real power lies in integrating and harmonizing your internal alpha and receptive energies, allowing you to act in a balanced, truly effective way.

In Chinatown all those years ago, Madame Woo's simple statement "I fix" had to do with balancing these energies within me so that they could perform their wondrous dance. She helped me heal my physical condition by using this principle of balancing giving and receiving energy, but I also learned that I could use it to manifest my dreams and desires and feel fulfilled. I still use my active dynamic energy, but when I brought in the receptive magnetic it was like the difference between a sixty-watt bulb and a crystal chandelier. I'd never felt so strong and vitalized—I felt like I'd just plugged in to the main line of the electric company!

Years later, as I was working toward my dream of having a child, my access to my magnetic energy served me in several ways. First, as soon as I let go of the idea that I needed a man to help me conceive and raise children, tremendous support began pouring into my life. My friends and family rallied around me. I opened myself up to receiving, and I was flooded with love and encouragement. Friends worked tirelessly to put together the nursery, do my grocery shopping, and hold my hand, telling me, "You can do this. I know you can."

By my fifth month of pregnancy, I needed that support even more. The twins' weight was resting on my sciatic nerve, and it was relentless and devastatingly painful, making it very hard for me to walk or sit down. Even a program of massage, stretching, yoga, swimming, and hot and cold packs could provide only a little bit of relief. Barely able to hobble across the room, I was forced to admit that I needed assistance even for little things. By opening to my magnetic energy, I was always able to draw to me someone who would quickly pick up an item I had dropped on the floor or help me in and out of a cab. Talk about feeling helpless and weak! But I knew I had to get over it and let others help me. I knew that as long as the babies were continually growing, their increasing weight would only put more pressure on an already aggravated condition, making it even more painful and difficult to move. All of my "can do" dynamic energy had been great for helping me get this far, but it was never so clear to me that two energies are better than one. Try an energy bath to bring them together.

Energy Bath: Bringing Together Your Magnetic and Dynamic Energies

As your bathtub begins to fill, pour in a few drops of rose oil, which will connect you to your magnetic energy, and a few drops of ylang-ylang oil, a stimulating oil that awakens your dynamic force. When your tub is full, place a soft bath pillow under your neck. Slide down into the water and immerse your body up to your neck, settling into a comfortable position.

Close your eyes and take a deep breath. Begin your Belly Breathing and pay attention to the feeling of your breath entering your body. As you exhale, feel your body let go of any tension that you are holding. Inhale deeply again, aware of the feeling of air being drawn into you. Exhale slowly. Continue inhaling and exhaling very slowly, and experience your body becoming more and more relaxed. Breathe, and release.

When you are feeling very calm, imagine a bright, shiny gold metallic ball a few feet in front of you to your right. Feel its energy radiating as its flames crackle and leap outward. Feel its warmth extending toward you. This is your dynamic energy.

Look to your left, a few feet in front of you, and see a silvery, metallic sphere, so shiny that it's like a ball of liquid mercury. Feel it pulling you, yearning to connect with your heart. This is your magnetic energy.

Sit and feel the energy of these balls of light and your connection to them. Breathe in, and feel their power. You are going to bring their power in to you, into your heart, alternating between pulling in the gold light and pulling in the silver light until they are both inside you.

Look to the golden orb and remember back to a time when

you felt strong and confident, a time when you went full speed ahead past any fear you had and did what you wanted to do. Experience that power and watch the golden orb as it comes closer in toward you.

Look to the silvery ball and remember back to a time when you attracted someone you desired or something you wanted. Experience that moment when it came to you, drawn in by your energy. See the silver ball come in closer . . . closer to your heart.

Look again to the golden orb and remember a time when you were disciplined and followed a plan to achieve a result. Experience your pride in having done it right, at having produced your results. As you experience this feeling, pull the orb closer in to your heart.

Look again to the silvery, magnetic ball as its energy swirls and remember a time when you allowed your creativity to form something new and beautiful. Experience the exhilaration of flexibility and creativity, the excitement of creation, as you pull your magnetic energy closer in to you.

Inhale, and as you do, draw both the shiny metallic silver ball and the golden orb fully into your heart. Exhale.

Feel the energies balancing each other as they do in a Yin and Yang symbol. See the silver and gold light integrate and shine brighter than ever, glowing with shared intensity. Experience this power. . . . Let it become a part of you.

Now, slowly, open your eyes.

You can take the first step toward reawakening your lost magnetic attraction right away with the following exercise. The more you do this exercise, the more you'll increase your ability to attract things to you, and you'll be amazed at what a difference it will begin to make in your life.

Become an Energy Magnet!

Think about a desire that came up for you in the desires and dreams exercise in Chapter 1, such as a fantastic job or your dream vacation. Whatever it is, begin to picture it in your mind.

Now, close your eyes and visualize a silver orb approximately six feet in front of your face. Breathe in and out, directing your breath into the silver orb. As you are breathing, picture what you desire within the silver orb. Feel as if you are a magnet drawing your desire from the orb to yourself. Let go of any thoughts or resistance about the impossibility of this desire, or feeling that you do not deserve this happiness. Allow and draw toward you the good feelings of having what you want permeate every cell of your body, feeling a sense of joy and well-being about having already received your heart's desires.

Believing and Receiving

Do you believe you're worthy of drawing the attention and appreciation of others? Sadly, many of us don't believe that we deserve happiness. This sense of deserving is born out of a true appreciation and acknowledgment of who you are and what you bring in to other people's lives just by being yourself. When you can realize the value of who you are and what you have to contribute, you will no longer take your innate talents for granted. You will be able to appreciate the uniqueness of yourself and the things you have to offer. You'll realize that wanting—and receiving what you want—doesn't mean that you are selfish; instead, your magnetic qualities will allow you to share and give to others. You will be able to acknowledge that you have needs and that they should be fulfilled in order for you to be happy. Most important, you'll realize that these needs are just as important as those of other people. No matter what you want to draw in, maintain, and foster, you *must* start with this feeling of entitlement. If you don't, you can work like a whirling dervish trying to make your dreams come true, but you will block your magnetic energy from helping you to receive it.

Do you find it difficult to believe that you deserve to have what you want? If so, I'd like you to try the following exercise.

"I Deserve to Receive"

Stand in the center of a room without shoes or socks on and take a deep breath in. Exhale. Do this three times, or until you feel relaxed. Then bend at the waist and place your hands on the floor. Imagine you are a tree with your roots reaching deep into the earth touching a pool of shiny, silver water. "Drink" up the water, pulling it upward, higher and higher, until it infuses your entire body. Feel this silver light illuminating you. Now, extend your hands outward with your palms facing up, as if you were opening yourself to receive.

Think of your desire and assertively say "I deserve." Continue proclaiming "I deserve . . ." as you keep your hands outstretched.

Notice whether the word *deserve* makes you feel uncomfortable and hesitant to say it, or if it's easy and fun to make your declaration. Notice, too, whether it's difficult for you to keep your hands outstretched in a receiving position, and if they feel weak or strong.

Some of my shyest, most soft-spoken clients were initially reticent about this exercise but now say they are comfortable with the feeling of power they get from asking for what they want and receiving it.

Try this exercise just before you have to make a dreaded phone call, confront someone, or speak in front of a group of people.

When you use your magnetic energy, you not only attract what you want, but you can retain it, foster it, build upon it, and increase it—all because you feel deep down that you are entitled to what you've gotten. A famous life coach admitted to me that at the beginning of his career, he let a million dollars slip away due to bad investments, saying, "I felt so unworthy of the wealth that I couldn't bring myself to look closely at my accounts or question my money manager." Once he got over this block and allowed himself to feel that he deserved his hard-earned wealth, he began making more money, investing it wisely, and growing his fortune.

The same thing happens with romantic relationships. If you don't start with the feeling that you're worthy of a fulfilling relationship, you will not attract the person who can create it with you, because you're blocking your magnetic energy. If you know what you want, you can start to be a player in life instead of sitting on the sidelines. It's been said before that self-confidence is the greatest aphrodisiac. When you feel and act like you deserve attention, men will be magnetically drawn to you.

Draw on Hidden Forces

Once your magnetic energy is awakened, hidden forces will come into play, drawing to you people and situations that can help you manifest your dreams.

I had a client, Danielle, who dreamed of living in a beautiful house on the ocean. "When I'm in nature," she told me, "it instantly shifts me to a calmer, more peaceful state. My soul just hungers for a connection to the natural world. But I'm stuck in a city apartment, miles from the ocean. I just wish I could have a beach house where I could smell the salty air and hear the pounding surf as I drift off to sleep. I want to take walks on the sand, listen to the seagulls, and look out at the horizon. But I can't possibly afford a down payment and a mortgage. I'd have to work every waking moment to make that kind of money."

"I know it *seems* impossible," I told her, "but by thinking that way, you're blocking yourself from drawing that house to you." I suggested that she regularly work with the "I Deserve" exercise to draw her house to her. I also encouraged her to repeat the following Power Mantra I wrote especially for her situation, "I deserve a beautiful beach house to live in and the money to afford it." I instructed her to say it as she was driving her car, whisper it under her breath when she was walking down the street, or even sing it in the shower. "As you say these words," I told her, "imagine this thought surrounded by a bubble of shimmering silver light. Or picture the house itself, with a silver glow around it."

Danielle followed my advice and even though results didn't happen right away she continued to do these exercises. And then one night when she was at a friend's party, she met a couple who were quite wealthy who told her that they'd lost money in the stock market and really wanted to start investing in real estate. As they talked, it became clear that this couple was willing to partner with Danielle to put a down payment on a house for her, and soon she was packing up her apartment and on her way to her new home: a beautiful beach house on the Atlantic.

It hadn't occurred to Danielle that there were financial resources available to her other than her own ability to make money, but by using the Life-Shift Tools of Color Immersion, Organic Breathing, Focused Reflection, and Power Mantras, she drew in the resources she needed to manifest her dream home.

When you are in your magnetic energy, anything that you previously thought was impossible turns out to be very possible. You will be tapping into the magnetic energy of universal support that will draw other people, resources, and avenues to you. What's more, everything that is drawn to you will come as part of the greater purpose of helping you get to the next level of realizing your dreams and, ultimately, your destiny.

Release How It's "Supposed to Happen"

If you truly believe you deserve to get and keep what you desire, you also have to release your need to control how it's going to come about. It's funny, but sometimes the very road you think is leading you away from fulfilling your deepest dreams and desires is actually the shortcut to them; you just can't see it at the moment. As my mother always used to say to me, "It's not good or bad till God gets through with it."

My client Lynn worked as a flight attendant, and she loved her job because it allowed her to travel the world, but she dearly wanted to get married and have a family of her own. When she came to me for healing sessions, she had been in a series of relationships with unavailable men and was very upset. "I feel like I'm never going to find true love, get married, and have a baby!" she said.

To cheer herself up, Lynn booked a ski vacation in France and told herself that maybe she'd find a man on the slopes. But just one day into her holiday, she called me from a hospital in Paris. Her voice cracked as she told me she'd broken her knee. "I can't believe my bad luck. My dream vacation just went down the tubes. I'm stuck here in a hospital bed! Why did I even bother coming to France?"

I told her I could certainly understand why she was upset, but to keep holding on to her dream of a husband and family, because the universe works in strange ways. Two days later, she decided that at the very least, she had to get out of her bed and hobble around the hospital a little. Adorned in her leg cast, she made her way to the recreation room and there she spotted a very handsome Frenchman, adorned in his own arm cast. They got to talking and laughed as they awkwardly tried to shoot pool. The chemistry was instantaneous.

I didn't hear from Lynn for about a year, but then she called me up, bursting with excitement. "I married that great guy from the hospital in Paris, and—well, next week our son is being christened! Can you believe it?"

Yes, I could, because I'd seen stranger things happen. "I guess your hospital stint wasn't a detour after all—it was a shortcut!" I said. As Lynn learned, if you believe that you deserve to receive, get in touch with your magnetic energy, focus on what you want, and keep your eyes peeled, you can see your dreams come true in the most unexpected ways.

There's a wonderful story about a man who was drowning. As he struggled against the waves that threatened to drag him under, he prayed to God, "Lord, please rescue me! I desperately need your help!"

Very soon, a schooner approached him, and its captain, seeing the man in distress, called out, "You there! Grab this life preserver and we'll pull you in!"

"No, that's okay," said the drowning man. "I have faith. God will rescue me."

The captain shook his head and sailed on.

Then a larger boat came by, and the skipper called out, "You there! Hold on—we'll lower a life raft and come get you!"

"No, that's okay," said the drowning man. "I have faith. God will rescue me."

The skipper and his mates were all surprised, but they shrugged their shoulders and steered the boat away.

Now, by this time the drowning man was quite weary, barely able to keep his head above water. He heard a helicopter overhead and looked up to see someone leaning out of the passenger side, holding a megaphone and shouting, "You there! Hold on, and I'll lower a ladder to you!"

"No, that's okay," the man said. "I have faith in God. He will rescue me."

And with that, the helicopter flew away.

As night began to fall, the drowning man at last was overcome with exhaustion and his head slipped below the surface.

All was dark, and then he suddenly realized he was in heaven, standing before the glorious light of God.

"Welcome, my son," said the Lord.

"God, it is so wonderful to be in your presence! I have been a religious man all my life, and I've always had faith that you would answer my prayers. But when I was drowning, you didn't come to rescue me. Why, oh Lord?"

"I didn't come to rescue you?!" said the Lord. "You didn't see the schooner? You didn't see the boat? You didn't see the helicopter?"

Just like the drowning man, when you're stuck in your own limited ideas about how your dreams are going to come true, you miss the boat and the helicopter too. But when you're flexible about how it's going to happen, you don't block the Magnetic Female energy. Start to recognize the signs of possibilities, and embrace them when they show up in ways other than how you had imagined.

The magnetic and dynamic energies create an awesome force, especially when they are complementing each other. When they are aligned, supporting your dreams, you will truly feel that what was once "impossible" is really quite possible. You will have the confidence to get motivated and begin your journey, while setting your intention so that the universe can help you go to the next level of joy and fulfillment. Your positive outlook will match your positive desires, and you will be intrinsically drawn toward the possible. At this point, there won't be anything that you can't have or become.

4

STEP TWO: CONNECTING THE
FOUR BODIES

December 29, 2000, the Inca Trail, Peru

When I decided to get pregnant, my friend Dana Kennedy invited me to take a trip with her along the Inca Trail, which leads to the lost city of Machu Picchu, high above the Andes in Peru. Dana is a journalist who had gone on many spiritual journeys, and she'd painted an enticing picture of a four-day hike to the ancient, sacred city. She'd described us sleeping under the stars in cozy sleeping bags. Porters would help us carry our provisions and cook us delicious meals along the way. I quickly told her to sign me up! I had heard about the amazing fertility herbs that grow in the Amazon jungle as well as the rituals performed by two highly revered Peruvian shamans. We'd contacted these priests before our trip, and they'd agreed to work with me. All we had to do was paddle up the Amazon and climb a mountain or two to make it happen. No problem when you're on the baby quest.

By the third day of hiking, there were plenty of problems. For most of the day, Dana galloped way ahead, leaving me alone. I hadn't listened to Dana's warning weeks ago, when she said, "Aleta, don't you think you'd better train for this hike?" I'd been working on a project and had had no time to put in for extra exercise, so I'd confidently assured her that I would be just fine. What had I been thinking? Now it was all I could do to catch my breath in the thin air, 13,650 feet above sea level. Then the skies opened up and rain suddenly began pouring down in sheets. As the porters gingerly passed me on the path, I got a glimpse of my "nice, cozy" sleeping bag and tent, now totally drenched. I was exhausted and wet, and the only thing I had to look forward to was sleeping in a cold, soggy sleeping bag, eating yet another meal of rice and beans.

I stared above me at a forbidding sign, DEAD WOMAN'S PASS, aptly named from the arrangement of the terrain, which is said to represent a woman lying on her back. The trail takes you over her belly and, as you pass over the top, there are two peaks said to resemble a woman's breasts. I wondered how many women had died climbing this treacherous trail, and would I be another?

My body heaved as I propped myself up on a stone ledge. As I rested in the pounding rain, my eyes caught the most magnificent vista: The green, grassy plains and majestic mountains were surrounded by a gauze of clouds. I let go and a feeling of calm and peace settled over me. I began to breathe deeper and more slowly. My body stopped complaining, my emotions took a chill, and my mind ceased its chatter. It was as if a basket of white feathers was coming down and brushing every part of me, and I knew that it was my spiritual self.

My spiritual self was merging with my body, mind, and emotions. I looked up at the sky, and everything started to expand. I sensed white light all around me and felt at one with the universe. I stood up and felt the white light vibrating through every cell in my body. Suddenly, my dynamic energy came alive, and I began putting one foot in front of the other as I used my magnetic energy to draw from this white light, which gave me the stamina to keep going. Before I knew it, I had caught up to Dana, much to the surprise of everyone on the trail.

While I'd expected great insight and a deeper integration to occur *when I got to Machu Picchu, it took place right on the trail. Even though I'd carefully mapped out my trip, I was going to have to let go of my plans, keep my intentions in mind, and let life take its course—and try not to look down the ravine and think about how if I slipped, I'd go bumping and sliding for thousands of feet. My journey made clear to me that to reach my goal, I had to surrender my preconceived notions about how my trip was going to happen and be in harmony with everything going on around me and within me.*

As I continued through the pass, I focused on my desire to become pregnant. I had been working to integrate my spiritual energy into every part of myself for decades, and was successfully teaching others to do it. I realized that in order to get pregnant, I had to work harder at aligning the four aspects of myself—the physical, emotional, mental, and spiritual— in order to fulfill my dream. On the Inca Trail, I learned that when I released my negative thoughts and feelings, it allowed each part of myself to connect with the divine energy of faith, belief, and manifestation, and I was able to get past my limitations. With this knowledge, I knew in my heart that I could work toward successfully conceiving.

Four Vibrating Bodies

I like to call the physical, emotional, mental, and spiritual aspects of each of us the Four Bodies. Imagine that your emotions, your thoughts, and your spiritual self are separate entities, housed within your physical body, like Russian nesting dolls. Because they're all sharing the same space, these four bodies influence one another. For instance, you can try to be as healthy as possible, to eat right and exercise, but if you're furious with a friend, it's going to affect your physical body. The anger in your emotional body will cause your physical body to release stress hormones that can fatigue you and weaken your immune system. Similarly, you can try your best to manage your emotions, but if your mind keeps bringing up thoughts like "I'm never going to reach my goals" and "I'm too old/too fat/too skinny/too lazy," you'll still experience painful feelings like fear, sadness, shame, and anger.

If it seems odd to imagine having a mental "self" that is vibrating, or to envision your physical body, which may be sitting still in a chair as you read this, think back to science class, when you learned about atoms and particles. Even though we seem to be solid creatures, we're actually made up of millions of invisible energy particles that are vibrating very quickly, like a swarm of bees. You can see the swarm—it looks almost solid from a distance—but it consists mostly of space, filled with fast-moving dots of energy. That's you— a buzzing, vibrating creature of immense energy. And each of your four bodies, layered one on top of another, is vibrating. These separate bodies create a network of interwoven perceptions, beliefs, and feelings that influence how we use our magnetic and alpha energies to create the life that we desire.

Your four bodies are like the octaves on a piano. The lowest octave, the one whose notes vibrate at a slower speed, is the physical body; the next octave up, with notes that vibrate at a slightly higher speed, is the emotional body; then comes the mental body; and, finally, the spiritual body, which has the fastest vibration. Just as with the highest octave on a piano, the spiritual body has the "highest frequency" (when it comes to musical notes, the faster the vibration, the "higher" the note sounds).

But a piano is nothing except furniture until someone plays it. And in order for it to make wonderful music, it first needs to be tuned. Each of us works in much the same way. By tuning each of your four bodies so that they vibrate together in glorious harmony, your Russian nesting dolls will come to life. You can manifest your dreams and desires through harmonizing your four bodies in concert with both your dynamic and magnetic energies.

When you harmonize the vibrational rates of your bodies, you'll increase your positive energy and exist in a higher consciousness. You'll be able to rise above difficulties instead of obsessing over problems. Being able to disengage and maintain a higher mindset and a positive attitude is absolutely crucial to any type of success. My clients find that when they do this, they're astonished at how quickly they're able to manifest their dreams and desires. So when someone casually says, "Oh, you're not still going on about opening your own restaurant, are you?" or "So when are you going to get married?" or "Aren't you too old to do that?" you won't have to use your valuable energy to manage a whirlwind of insecure thoughts and feelings.

When you are vibrating at a higher energy level, you are in the same field of energy as others who are vibrating at that higher level. You actually resonate to them, attract them, and harmonize with them. For example, when a flock of birds suddenly shifts direction, all the birds are able to turn at once. Because they are sharing the same energy field, they are connected, and they resonate with one another. When one bird decides to shift direction, the other birds instantaneously feel that shift in energy and move at the same time. It's almost magical.

If you are vibrating at this higher rate most of the time, even if you slip to a lower vibration, your fall won't last for long. No one is perfect, and I still have moments when I get derailed. However, now I'm able to quickly get back on track and devote my energy to creating the things I want in my life instead of creating more of what I don't want.

So how do you reach and maintain a higher consciousness? You need to start by getting rid of the negativity that is lodged in the cells of your body that can weigh you down. You know the feeling you get when you are constipated: You are physically blocked up and nothing can pass through your system. Just as your physical body is made sluggish, your mental body is dragged down by dark thoughts, and your emotional body is slowed by negative emotions like anger and fear. These blocks can keep us enmeshed in old negative beliefs, emotional struggles, disappointments, and angers. Your spiritual body, which vibrates at a very high rate, doesn't get polluted with toxins, but you can't make the most of its marvelous force if your other three bodies are blocked. By clearing the toxins that are in your physical, emotional, and mental bodies, you can harmonize them with your spiritual body and vibrate at a higher rate. This creates an exquisite concert of music, bringing your dreams to miraculous fruition. I promise.

To be successful, you need to release these blocks and let your positive energy flow. Let's start with the largest nesting doll, which surrounds the others: the physical body.

The Physical Body

Your physical body is an extraordinary mechanism, with a multitude of very complex systems all working to support one another. Your body is strong, with tremendous potential for healing itself, yet at the same time it's fragile and vulnerable. If you've ever had an operation, sustained an injury, or recovered from a horrible flu, you know what I am talking about. You can be enthusiastic and committed to realizing your dreams, but if you're neglecting your body, you will have to devote an enormous amount of energy just to remain healthy and alert. You won't have the energy to create and maintain success in your life.

Healthy Breathing

If you are under stress, or are worried, angry, or anxious, you can have a tendency to hold your breath or breathe shallowly. This creates a buildup of toxins in your body because you're not inhaling enough oxygen to feed your cells, and you're not exhaling deeply either, so you're not releasing enough carbon dioxide. Deeper breathing allows you to quickly recenter and energize yourself, draw in plenty of oxygen, and exhale toxins.

Here is a breathing exercise that I learned from a very powerful Peruvian shaman whom I worked with in the Amazon jungle. He taught me how to start expanding my lungs in order to increase my body's capacity to take in oxygen, which, in turn, cleans toxins.

> Imagine that your breath is a wave in the ocean. As the wave comes in toward shore, you take a deep breath and inhale, holding it for a moment and then exhaling as the wave recedes. As you visualize the wave coming in again, you inhale deeply, hold the breath, and as the wave recedes, exhale once again. Practice this exercise consciously and fully, and you will experience your lung capacity and stamina increasing.

Eat Right

If you want your physical body to operate at its highest frequency, you need to start by making sure your cells have plenty of revitalizing nutrients. Choose foods that nurture your body, and choose them regularly. Eat a balanced diet that contains a mixture of proteins, fruits and vegetables, grains, and some dairy, avoiding foods you know aren't good for you.

You might say, "Aleta, I'm already eating very healthfully!" If that's so, take this challenge anyway, because your definition of healthy eating may not be so healthy after all. Good-quality foods can be a vital source of energy. There are foods that are used to increase your energy, like proteins and whole grains, and there are foods that are used to cleanse and move your energy, such as vegetables and fruits. Junk foods, especially those with refined sugars, have a low vibrational rate and clog up the movement of your energy. The higher vibrational foods—whole, fresh foods—bring your body up to the frequency that harmonizes with your higher spiritual self. As you increase your vibrational rate and start eating better, you will magnetically be drawn toward better foods, and you will choose them without hesitation or feeling deprived.

Take out your journal and write down everything you eat every day for an entire week. You might be surprised at how much junk food you consume. I had a client who thought she was eating healthy because she ate so many salads, but she'd glop on a half cup of creamy dressing, loads of bacon bits, and a pile of greasy croutons, never realizing that she might as well have treated herself to her favorite fast-food hamburger instead.

If you feel tired all the time and always seem to be under the weather, it's probably because you're not being completely honest about your eating habits. Eating high-quality, nutritious foods every day will make a remarkable difference in your energy level. My client Rose was sixty years old and dearly wanted to go back to school and earn a master's degree in child psychology, but she was afraid to apply to a program. "If I get in," she told me, "how can I possibly handle all those classes and the homework? I'll be wiped out!" I encouraged Rose to start eating better. She cut out fried foods and greasy, salty foods, and learned to love fresh vegetables, fresh fruits, whole grains, and proteins. Eating this way, Rose started to feel much more energetic, and she was able to go for her dream and earn her degree.

One of the main criticisms I received about having twins at fifty-seven was that I wouldn't have enough stamina to raise my children. That would be true if I didn't continue to eat right and exercise, in which case I wouldn't have the vigor to keep up with my kids.

Changing your eating habits for the better will let you run at peak performance and catapult you past any age barriers you perceive. And for those of you who are still smoking, I think you know what I'm going to say . . . ! I know it's tough. I had to let go of my dear friend the cigarette.

Before starting any new kind of eating program, it's important to check it out with your physician. If you've had a digestive problem you've been ignoring for a long time, or have recurring headaches or chronic pain, it's time to check out what is going on instead of just living with it. You might be surprised to learn that a simple change—like eliminating certain foods from your diet and adding others—can make a huge difference in how you feel.

Cleanse Your Internal Systems

When you eat right (even most of the time) and exercise, your body will naturally get rid of toxins that are blocking your system. However, even the best intentions can backfire. Before my pregnancy, I ate well and avoided toxins like caffeine and refined sugar. Even so, I discovered that a lot of heavy metals, such as lead and mercury, had built up in my blood. I was totally shocked because I thought I was being so good! But I learned that just living in polluted New York City and having deep-water fish as a staple of my diet were the culprits. This could very well have been a factor in my miscarriages.

There are many ways you can unclog your internal systems. I took detoxifying herbal supplements and made even more of an effort to drink freshly squeezed vegetable juices because they not only gave my body valuable nutrients, they also helped my detoxifying organs—my liver, gallbladder, and kidneys—to function more efficiently. Wheatgrass is a wonder for balancing blood sugar and alkalizing your body.

Keeping your colon as clean as possible is really important. The goal is to keep your body and your digestive system moving at all times. As you dynamically take in food, your magnetic energy draws out the nutrients that you need and starts to move the waste through the body. When you have accumulated more waste material, it creates blockages in your system. Physical matter is your densest matter. When you are bogged down with physical waste, you can't use your energy to its highest potential.

I went through a process called chelation, which draws out metals from your body. I also saw a colon therapist, whose job it is to keep your body as clean and alkaline as possible. When there is too much acid in your system, diseases begin to grow.

A first step is to make sure that you are getting the proper amounts of fiber-rich foods and the recommended doses of minerals. This includes taking in proper amounts of calcium, magnesium, vegetables, vegetable juices, and wheatgrass, as well as limiting your intake of acidic foods and beverages like sodas and coffee. There are test kits to see if your body is really acidic, and these are commonly found at health food stores.

As your body starts to dump toxins, you'll probably have a few days of feeling absolutely horrible. You may experience your old aches and pains again, and you'll hate me for even suggesting these changes. But suddenly you'll feel a significant shift: Your body will feel incredibly revitalized, you'll have a renewed sense of well-being, and your thinking will become much clearer. For instance, one of my clients discovered that when she simply stopped drinking diet soda for breakfast, she had much more vigor, her mood improved, and her skin glowed.

Water Is the Real Elixir of Life

You can start revving up your body simply by making a commitment to drink at least eight glasses of water a day. Water is the primary way that you can help flush out toxins. Replace acidic coffee with healthier green tea, which still has caffeine but is better for you (be sure to cut down on coffee gradually or you'll get sick to your stomach and feel like a hammer is banging against your head).

You can start cleansing your internal house right away, getting rid of the toxins clogging your system, with my Quick Water Detox.

Quick Water Detox

In the morning, before you eat your breakfast, drink an eight-ounce glass of warm water with two tablespoons of lemon juice. This is a full-body detoxifying cleanse to help all your systems flush out any toxins. By drinking this every day, you begin your day with a clean feeling. When people have a clean feeling, their energy comes through in a pure form. Their intentions are not as clogged with the constipated feeling of holding everything in.

Get Moving

You can quickly feel a change in energy when you exercise. Getting your blood circulating through stretching, building, and toning your muscles will support your body in staying young, healthy, and energetic. Your sex life doesn't have to be over when you turn forty, fifty, or sixty. You don't have to lose your attractiveness and your vitality just because the years are passing. I have lots of clients who, like me, look better now than they did in their thirties, and there's a reason for it—they're not couch potatoes.

Exercise not only creates but also moves energy. When you are exercising your body, you are detoxifying your entire body. At the same time, you are allowing your body to magnetically draw in more oxygen so that your physical body becomes more efficient. Your muscles become stronger and more flexible when both your dynamic and magnetic energies are working together.

Doctors say that exercise decreases your chance of heart attacks, stroke, high cholesterol, high blood pressure, and osteoporosis. Studies show that regular exercise and stretching will also help you shift out of depression and create a better attitude. When you get your heart pumping faster as you stretch, run, or swim, your body releases endorphins that lift your mood and spirits and help you to think more clearly. I have a client who simply stopped taking the elevator up to her apartment every day and walked ten flights of stairs instead. She noticed a remarkable difference in her overall energy level, and her figure transformed to "hot babe" status.

If you loathe exercise, try doing it while you listen to your favorite upbeat music on an iPod or Walkman, or crank up your stereo to help you break through that resistance. Take a walk to buy healthy food, or tape your favorite TV show and only allow yourself to watch it if you work out while it's playing.

Before starting any new exercise program, get a checkup by your doctor to make sure that all your systems are in order. If you haven't exercised in a long time, start slowly. Find an exercise program that works for you, your temperament, and your lifestyle. Some people do better with classes, others with workout tapes they use at home, and others prefer to combine their exercise with getting outdoors and socializing.

If you're new to exercise, make a plan that's realistic for you. Overdoing it will just cause you to become injured, experience the pain of sore muscles, and grow discouraged, and you'll be tempted to stop. Do as much as feels comfortable for you, but the most important thing is that you do *something* at least three times a week. If you are starting out and you keep going for at least three days a week for each of the next three weeks, your body will start to love it and urge you to keep going. When you feel vital, energized, and at peace, everything seems possible . . . and it is.

Quick Detox Workout

The next time you feel really tired or stressed out, start lifting your mood immediately through exercise. Spend twenty to thirty minutes dancing, biking, stretching, or whatever gets you moving. Don't worry about reaching your maximum heart rate or counting calories burned: You'll know you're doing it right if you break a sweat and have to struggle a bit to have enough breath to carry on a conversation. It's important to perspire, because your skin, with all of its pores and sweat glands, is your biggest detoxifying organ.

After you're finished with your Quick Detox Workout, take a long, hot shower. Visualize all the sugar, fat, and artificial coloring from that doughnut you ate the other night being washed away with your sweat, spiraling down the drain. After you dry off and get dressed, sit for a while and just feel the sensations in your body. Feel your blood circulating. Feel your heart beating steadily at a calm pace. Feel how quiet your thoughts have become. Sit in this experience of peace and serenity, savoring it.

You might say, "Aleta, that all sounds great, but I'm really too busy. I can't fit exercise into my life." The busier you are, the more important it is to de-stress. An hour of exercise three times a week followed by stretching will make a huge difference—you will be healthier and feel invigorated. You deserve to make some time for yourself and give yourself this incredible gift of health and energy.

I know that the older one gets, the harder it is to make lifestyle changes. It's easier to follow the same routine and settle into things. But as we get older, if we don't keep moving and stretching, we will start deteriorating. Without internal and external movement, our bodies can crystallize where they are. I challenge myself and my clients, and now you, to do things that are new and exciting in order to get out of your comfort zone. That is why I like taking people away on spiritual travel adventures where nothing is familiar. They have to be open to all kinds of experiences that come in: eating different kinds of foods, getting up at different times, not having their creature comforts next to them. And that's when they really life shift.

While I know it's probably hard for you to get on a plane and meet me on the Inca Trail, I want you to think about how you can start something new with your body, and see what life shift will follow.

A Love Note to Your Body

To keep my clients' food, exercise, and detox plans realistic, I ask them to write a love note to their body outlining what they're going to do for the coming week. For instance, every Sunday night I sit down and write a letter and put it on my refrigerator. It goes something like:

"Dear Body, Thank you for serving me. This week I promise to exercise you for thirty minutes or more on Monday, Wednesday, and Saturday; drink green tea instead of coffee in the morning; cut down on refined sugars and focus on whole grains, proteins, and eat at least two dark green vegetables and a raw salad every day. And I won't be so hard on you."

My clients find this a fun and effective way to remind themselves to stick to their plan. It's amazing to me that these types of small lifestyle changes really can make a big difference. So write your body a letter or incorporate these small, achievable goals into your dynamic energy–inspired to-do list.

Educating yourself can make such a difference in the goals that you set for yourself. As Maya Angelou says, "When you know better, you do better." Use the Web as a tool, visit a nutritionist—draw upon the resources out there to teach yourself how to take care of your body and find a food plan that works for you. The dedicated specialists I worked with during my pregnancy were part of what I began to call "Team Aleta," and they continue to be crucial supporters, helping me to stay healthy and vital.

Baths

Your mother was right: Cleanliness is next to godliness. A great, quick energy bath to help you release negative toxins will leave you feeling clean and refreshed. Just add about a cup of Epsom salts to your bathwater. Epsom salts can be bought anywhere, including your local supermarket, and are well known to revitalize your body. Soak for twenty minutes to get the full effect. It works like a charm to relieve sore muscles (from all the exercise you will be doing).

The Emotional Body

Once you have cleared the toxins from your physical body, it will be easier for you to address the next layer: your emotional body. Your emotional body is the gatekeeper to the physical, mental, and spiritual bodies. When the emotional body is out of balance, it has a direct effect on the health of your physical body and it blocks your mental body from maintaining a positive, unlimited perspective.

Getting in Touch with the Emotional Body

Early in my acting career, I was afforded the opportunity to really get in touch with my emotional body. Even though I could always tap into my emotions when I was playing a character, in my personal life I taught myself to hold back. I was proud of the fact that no one ever knew what I was really feeling. One day my good friend Thurman Scott, who was well known for helping actors quickly get into the heart of their characters and emotionally move audiences, was conducting an acting workshop and invited me to join.

As I approached the studio, I heard loud screaming. Gingerly, I climbed the stairs, and when I got to the landing, I realized that the screams were coming from Thurman's studio. I cautiously opened the door and came upon a scene that was like something out of *One Flew Over the Cuckoo's Nest*. All around me, people were rocking, screaming, crying, and even laughing. I wanted to quickly turn around and go home, but I hesitated for a moment, long enough for Thurman to see me and motion for me to come in.

I realized there was no graceful way to ignore my friend, so I smiled awkwardly and walked over to the edge of the room. Thurman came over and laid down a very thin bed sheet on top of the old, worn-out, and soiled carpet, gestured for me to lie down, and then he walked away. As I lay on my back, I just hoped that I wouldn't catch any diseases. I glanced over at another actor working with Thurman, who was urging him to "go deeper" as he pounded a pillow and shouted, "I hate you! I hate you!" I thought, "Oh, brother, he expects me to start wailing like a lunatic too?"

After what felt like an eternity of lying on my sheet, staring at the ceiling, and being barraged by sound, I gradually began to feel my emotions surfacing. To my surprise, I started to express them in a stream of consciousness that came from places inside of me that I never knew existed. It was strange and intense. Suddenly I felt like I was four years old, watching my father sail away as his ship left the dock. I remembered waving good-bye to him, crying and yelling, "Bad ship! Bad ship!" My whole body began shaking. One part of me was experiencing the trauma of my father leaving, while another seemed to have floated out of my body so that I could watch what was happening. I was taken aback by how strong my long-buried feelings of abandonment and rejection were. I had never allowed myself to feel, let alone express, them before. I'd always been the strong soldier who held my family together with the attitude of, "I can take care of everything and everyone."

Thurman came over and helped me express what I'd felt as a child and was reexperiencing. I found out that I had blamed my mother for my father's leaving, and felt that if my father had loved me enough, he would have stayed. Finally, it made perfect sense to me why I was always the giver and accommodator in relationships with men. Because my father had so often left to go to sea, I was afraid that men would leave me if I asked for what I needed and stopped taking care of them. I instantly realized that these childish thoughts and feelings were irrational, but they'd lodged themselves deep within me and I was still acting on them.

Once I felt my hurt and anger toward my father, a feeling of love for him immediately stirred up inside of me, creating a sense of security and peace in my heart that I had never experienced before. Again, my emotions surprised me, as I realized just how much love I had repressed underneath those feelings of grief and anger that I'd buried so long ago.

After that extraordinary evening, I was able to receive and feel the love my father had for me and, as a result, began to have more balanced relationships with the men in my life. As an added bonus, I lost five pounds over the next week without even trying. Could it be that my emotions had been making my body retain extra weight as a way of protecting myself from letting out my feelings of anger and hurt?

"Old Stuff" and Repressed Emotions

Negative feelings are toxins that must be released from the emotional body. When these feelings are trapped, they lower your vibration rate, keep you exhausted, lower your immunity, and can even make you physically ill. These are also symptoms of depression. This makes sense because depression often involves holding back or holding on to many dark feelings, such as fear and anger. When you hold these feelings in without releasing or transforming them, you do not have the energy to get past them. Sometimes depression forces you into an awkward stillness: You can't physically move, and you are emotionally paralyzed.

For example, one of my clients, Alison, frequently moved homes when she was a child and went through a hard time adjusting to new schools and making new friends. As an adult, whenever she was faced with changes, even ones she wanted to happen, she felt very anxious and even sick to her stomach, fearing that the outcome would be traumatic.

When you're going through stress due to changes, rejection, or loss, overwhelming emotions can rise up like waves from deep within. As you experience rage, shame, or any other negative emotion, it can trigger memories of emotional wounds from the past. You actually reexperience the original wounding as you connect your feelings from the past to your feelings in the present, and this intensifies your emotions. Suddenly, no matter how strong or intelligent you are, you feel as if you're a powerless little child, pulled down by the undertow of anxiety, insecurities, resentments, and hopelessness.

Often, we try to talk ourselves out of our emotions, pretending that we're really not that upset, but in doing so we just repress them, pushing them deeper into the subconscious. This not only stores the emotional toxins in your emotional body, it negatively affects your physical body as well. According to *Healing Back Pain* by John E. Sarno, M.D., "Pain in the back, neck, shoulders, and limbs is not caused by structural abnormalities but by the mind's effort to repress emotions." He believes that the mind tricks you into not facing repressed emotion by making you focus on pain in the body.

Even if you make a serious effort not to repress negative emotions and deal with them as they come up, you may find yourself giving in to them because these negative emotions *seem* to protect us from pain. One of my clients, Joan, made this mistake. She's a very sensitive person and her husband, Tom, was a very sarcastic guy. Tom's attempts to help Joan "lighten up" by making flippant comments made her feel hurt and disrespected, and she perceived his straightforward and often tactless advice as an attempt to boss her around.

Recognizing that they had a communication problem, Tom agreed to go to marital counseling with Joan. He began to change the way he talked to Joan, but she had so much hurt built up inside that she couldn't move on. She bought into the idea that if she remained angry and kept punishing Tom, she'd keep his sarcastic tendencies in check, and she wouldn't get hurt again. As soon as Tom did something nice or thoughtful, Joan would think about something he said in the past that she felt was deeply offensive, let herself get angry again, and remind him of how badly he used to behave. Tom would feel like he couldn't do anything right, would lose heart and stop trying to treat her well. Then Joan would criticize him even more, fearful that he would revert to his old behavior if she didn't stay mad at him.

What Joan didn't recognize was that by hanging on to the anger and reigniting it with her memories, she was stopping the positive energy from flowing, shutting down any movement in their relationship. It didn't prevent her from being hurt, but it did prevent her from moving forward and experiencing a loving, intimate relationship.

When we hold on to feelings of hurt, rejection, anger, or sorrow, we close down emotionally. We don't allow our minds to open up to the potential of different circumstances and situations. Instead of seeing a chance for love, we see a chance for rejection; instead of seeing a chance for trust, we see a chance for betrayal. The sad thing is that we shut down our emotions in order to escape any possibility of getting hurt again, but as you saw with Joan, that doesn't work, and while we're shutting down, we also block ourselves from positive emotions. We start to feel lonely and disconnected from ourselves and others.

Experiencing the pain is a necessary part of the process of releasing your feelings and healing your emotional body. As Marianne Williamson says, "What you don't feel, you can't heal."

I know you might be thinking, "Aleta, you don't know the pain I've been through. I just don't want to go there." But you're spending an enormous effort to keep those emotions buried. If you're afraid, behind your feeling of fear you've got a huge amount of power that you can free up to use for manifesting your deepest dreams and desires. It really is worth experiencing the pain and anger so you can release it.

As you release your emotional toxins and heal your old wounds you'll stop constantly reacting to the emotional traumas from your past. Remembering upsetting events will be like remembering when you were suffering from the worst flu you've ever had—you'll have a detached, unemotional response to the memory. And as you experience new feelings that may unsettle you, you'll be able to shift back into a more positive state rapidly and not need to dredge everything up from the past.

Of course, this will take practice and time, but I promise that you will start seeing results right away. To heal your emotional body, you've got to get out of your head. Sometimes, negative emotions well up in us so rapidly and so intensely that we don't even know what it is we're feeling. I've found this happens a lot with people who were brought up in families where anger was either not accepted at all or was the order of the day. The people I know who weren't allowed to express their anger as children immediately transmute that difficult emotion into sadness or despair, because those feelings were more acceptable in their homes. Other people who were brought up in families where anger was used to cover up hurt, embarrassment, and fear will create turmoil for themselves, raging against the world because the feeling of anger is familiar and less scary than the emotions that were taboo in their families. So often, we got such confusing messages about difficult emotions when we were growing up that when we feel ourselves upset in some vague way, we can't articulate it.

Releasing and Transforming the Emotional Body

The emotional blocks that prevent us from getting what we truly desire are deep and were not formed in one day. They will take time to clear. The following exercise will help you put your finger on what it is you're feeling so that you can use Color Immersion and Organic Breathing to release it. Use the following exercise anytime you feel challenged by your negative emotions.

Clearing Strong Emotions

When an intense, negative emotion suddenly gets you in its grip, the first thing to do is to slow down your breathing. When we panic, we either start breathing more quickly and shallowly or we hold our breath. When this happens, we suppress emotions. So if you're going to release these feelings instead of repressing them, you have to change your breathing.

Sit down and take a deep, slow breath, using your Connective Breathing technique. As you exhale, place your hand over your heart and let your emotions surface. As you continue to breathe deeply and slowly, ask yourself, "What am I feeling?" If you feel confused by what it is you're feeling and you can't articulate it, tell yourself, "I have the words for this feeling," and they will come to you.

Continue breathing deeply and slowly until you can identify what you are feeling. If you're feeling angry, envision a bright orange sun about a foot in front of you and inhale its rays into your heart. Exhale the feeling of anger outward into the sun and watch it burn up. Breathe in again and ask yourself what the fear is beneath the anger. Let the answer surface, then exhale the feelings of fear into the sun and continue doing this until the feeling dissipates and you have a sense of inner calm and balance. If you're feeling confused, the sun you picture should be cobalt blue, and if you're sad, make it hot pink. You can also use your Release Breathing and hold your negative feelings to the count of five before you release them into your chosen sun and breathe that color back into your heart center.

Bathe in Your Emotions

Nothing helps bring up emotions like a good, hot bath. While you're running the water, add a few drops of rose or geranium oil to help release the blocks and heal your emotional body. As you immerse yourself in the water, feel that the negative memories of the past are floating to the surface and evaporating. Take a good, long soak and visualize how you might feel if you were free from old wounds, and could start a new life today.

Your Mental Body

Your mental body houses your intellect. It is where you store conceptual distortions and misconceptions of how you feel about yourself, your possibilities, and the world around you. These distortions lower your vibrational rate and limit your creative possibilities by impeding your alpha and magnetic energies from working together.

Your thoughts are actually electrical energy created in your brain. You may have heard the term *neural connections*—these are the biochemical "wires" that get created as you experience life. A baby's brain forms neural connections at an astonishing rate, as it first starts to use its senses, seeing the world, smelling and tasting the foods it's exposed to, being touched, hearing its mother's voice, and so on. Every day when I watch Francesca and Gian start to interact with their world, I'm in awe of how quickly they are forming neural connections and starting to develop their brains.

How We Form Belief Systems

The energy from your thoughts shapes your life, how you experience it, and what you believe. With every thought you create, the electric grid in your brain is busy sending messages and forming new connections. Once your brain creates an idea, it is imprinted onto your subconscious. Your subconscious mind doesn't argue or reconsider the information; it just accepts it as a fact and files it away, permanently saving it on your mental "hard drive."

For instance, if you've experienced betrayal, you file away the simple thought "I just can't trust anyone," and over time you may build on it, adding negative thoughts that reinforce that belief. In this way, you have created a negative belief system. Soon, you've layered on thoughts like "Men are only out for one thing," "You have to be a liar and a cutthroat to succeed," and "Everyone has an ulterior motive." These negative belief systems are what I call Mental Toxins, and they stop you from drawing in to your life the happiness you desire.

Thoughts actually affect us at a molecular level, as scientific researcher Dr. Masaru Emoto, author of *The Hidden Messages in Water,* has discovered. His astonishing photographs of ice crystals show that water that has been exposed to positive words forms exquisite, complex snowflake patterns that are brightly illumined, whereas water exposed to negative words forms distinctly asymmetrical structures and crystals that are dimly visible under a microscope. Considering that our bodies are actually composed of 80 percent water, just imagine how your thoughts are affecting your body.

Now you can see how words have power! Think of what would happen if in a marathon the spectators began to shout, "You'll never make it!" "Nobody cares!" or "You're too old and tired to do this!" rather than enthusiastically cheering the runners on to the finish line.

Your thoughts direct energy toward manifestation. You can control and direct whether that energy is positive or negative. The way you express yourself matters not only to you (in terms of how you view your life), but to the universe. What words do you use to describe yourself and your life? Do you tell yourself and the people around you, "I'll always be heavy because I have no willpower!" or

"I'll never get this job"? Many people, if truly conscious of what they say in the span of any given day, would find that too many of their thoughts are negative. Scientific research has determined that the brain thinks one hundred thousand thoughts a minute, and that for many people up to 80 percent of those thoughts are negative. Eighty percent! These negative thought patterns and belief systems stain your outlook with negativity and can transform dreams into nightmares.

Power Mantras for Overcoming the Monkey Mind

The negative thoughts that hold down your mental body can start small, but they have amazing ways of building up. Getting stuck in your head and letting your thoughts spin out of control is what the Buddhists call giving in to the "monkey mind," and it's very easy to go there, especially when you're thinking negatively. If you harbor feelings of nondeserving, guilt, unforgiveness, fear of rejection, and failure, these clogged emotions prevent your Magnetic Feminine from attracting and drawing to you what you desire and dream of, derailing you from fulfilling your personal destiny.

If negative thoughts tend to slip into your mind, release them into a gold sun and repeat the appropriate Power Mantra to replace them. For instance, Helena told me that despite how busy she was with Thanksgiving preparations, in all sorts of odd moments angry thoughts and feelings about her estranged sister kept popping up. As she snapped green beans, she'd suddenly think, "My sister is ruining the holiday! Why did she have to stir up trouble?"

I told Helena that every time one of these thoughts popped into her mind, she should take a minute to breathe and release it into the gold light and repeat to herself, "My family is having a terrific Thanksgiving and we're happy to be together." I pointed out to

✦ 96 ✦

her that her thoughts were all about the past and that this Power Mantra would bring Helena back to the present. She couldn't do anything about her sister, but changing her own thoughts would change her energy, and that would give Helena a much better chance of manifesting that wonderful holiday and family gathering she wanted.

Notice how quickly your attitude changes when you release and let go, replacing your negative mantras with positive ones, and how excited you feel about manifesting your desires.

By using the Life-Shift Tool of Power Mantras, it gets easier and easier to pull yourself away from negative beliefs and imprint positive thought patterns on your subconscious. As positive thought patterns become more familiar to you, you'll start to reinforce them. The difference in your life will be huge. It'll be like you're dating a real prince instead of some guy who breaks dates at the last minute and thinks Valentine's Day is just a marketing ploy. Positive thoughts are so powerful and encouraging that the more you think them, the more you'll be inspired to do the work of shifting your thoughts from negative to positive every time. If you discover your prince is really a frog, you will have the courage to say "Ciao for now."

Here are a few more Power Mantras that will help you life shift away from negative thoughts to positive desires:

- ✦ My dreams are delayed, not denied.
- ✦ It hasn't happened *yet,* but I know it will.
- ✦ I am victorious over my obstacles.
- ✦ There's a divine timing that's working for me NOW!

As you continue to work through my program, you are beginning to experience what the physical body has realized: In order for it to feel strong, it needs energy drawn from the mental and emotional bodies. The emotional body realizes it needs the support of the physical and mental bodies to be balanced. Lastly, the mental body needs the clean fuel of the physical body and the encouragement of the emotional body to work at its highest potential. When all of these bodies are vibrating in harmony with one another, you can easily accept the energy of the spiritual body.

Your Spiritual Body

Before you were born, your spiritual body set up a stage and cast the players that would help you grow. Consider that your spiritual body actually created your physical, emotional, and mental bodies, assigning them the exact attributes and personality you need to fulfill your destiny. Is it possible that our spiritual body might have decided on the parents we'd be born to, our purpose in life, and the issues we would need to work on?

In many ancient religious writings, the spiritual body is referred to as a "light body." Vibrating at an extremely high frequency, your spiritual body surrounds your three other bodies, ready to be called in to saturate them with light. When the three bodies are able to receive its magnificence, it shines its light even more brightly. Some say the spiritual body reveals itself as an aura that glows above and around you, similar to those beautiful paintings of Jesus shown with a golden halo around him, radiating outward.

The spiritual body has the capacity to flow into your other bodies, harmonizing them, raising your vibration, and allowing you to be the most positive, energetic person you can be. But, unfortunately, many of us live long stretches of our lives disconnected from this wonderful power source. Any act that is selfish, greedy, and unkind is based in fear and disconnects us from that power, making it difficult for us to feel filled with light.

Without that feeling, we have trouble being grateful, and we focus instead on what we don't have. We have to struggle to be loving toward others, because we can't access the compassion our spirit has in abundance. But when we connect to our spiritual body, positive emotional feelings come easily and naturally. Like a beacon shining into the darkness, our spiritual bodies have the power to illuminate us.

The Experience of Connecting

The experience of connecting to our spiritual body feels a little different for everyone. For some people, it's as if they are weightless, not really connected to the room they're in or the chair they're sitting on. My client Sandy describes it as being immersed in a cosmic bathtub, and feeling connected to the stars and the planets and all of space. It can be a feeling that you're truly lit from within or a deep sense that every event you are observing has been carefully scripted, and the play is unfolding before you exactly as it's supposed to. Another client of mine, Melanie, says that when she gets in touch with her spiritual body through daily meditation, she finds herself inside a beautiful mental space, free of any worries or fears, and aware that anything is possible.

There are many ways to access the spiritual body. Sandy closes her eyes and turns her focus inward, then begins thinking of luminescent white light, the color most connected to spirituality. She even keeps a clean white card in her wallet, just to remind herself to connect to her spiritual body. Julianne says she pretends she's an angel, and then she imagines soft white wings coming out of her body.

Lindsey says that for her, the feeling of being connected to her spiritual body reminds her of the first few moments in the morning when you're switching over from a sleeping to a waking state. She describes her spiritual body as being her "best self," and she makes a point upon waking to check in on the state of all of her bodies. She asks herself if her mental body is taking over with thoughts about what she has to accomplish today. Is her emotional body giving in to worry, fearing that she won't get through her to-do list? Can she feel her spiritual body or is she disconnected from it? Does her physical body feel right and at ease? After checking in with her bodies, she takes a deep breath, releases any negative thoughts or feelings, and reconnects with her best self if she needs to. Then, throughout the day, she checks back to see if she's gotten disconnected again, letting people or work get to her. If so, she releases the feelings and thoughts and again reconnects.

Often, if you have experienced a great loss, you may find that the connection to your spiritual body feels out of reach. When Becky first entered my studio, she was wearing her workout gear and looked like she'd walked right out of a Nike commercial. One would think that she had men falling at her feet. She was effervescent, enthusiastic, and optimistic about life and her possibilities—at least on the surface. But my intuition sensed that deep inside her, Becky's heart was closed, and that she had suffered a very grave wound. Her sorrow was so palpable, I felt myself tearing up. I took her hand and said, "You're experiencing very deep sadness. It feels like it's connected to a relationship."

With that, Becky's demeanor switched immediately. I could feel her pain as she talked about her past. Two years earlier her husband had died in a car crash, leaving her to deal with the financial and emotional pressure of raising four children on her own. Her grief and sense of shock were so great that even though she'd had what she called a "very strong relationship with God," she had blocked herself off from it. "I just can't resolve how God could take away my husband. We loved each other so much. He was such a good man and a good father to his children."

Over time, we worked together, releasing pain from her physical, emotional, and mental bodies. Finally, Becky had a breakthrough. In one of our sessions, she pointed to a spot six inches above her navel and said, "Aleta, I feel as if there's a little black stick figure in my solar plexus." The solar plexus represents our power center, and I instantly knew that this black figure represented her, so I decided to focus on helping her get rid of the biggest emotional toxin she had—her anger toward God. As we worked with Organic Breathing and Color Immersion, Becky said, "It's changing. The figure! It's becoming emerald green. It's like looking at my babies for the first time." She began to cry. "It's so beautiful."

She was letting her spiritual body come alive again after two years of shutting itself off deep inside of her.

"I feel like I have an energy body of light underneath my skin and it's pulsating and moving through my whole body!" she exclaimed.

Filled with this extraordinary force, Becky finally felt able to release her anger at God for taking her husband, and a deep feeling of peace and calm came over her. She had reconnected to God and to her own spiritual body and felt that she could start living her life again.

Power Prayers Connect You with the Spiritual Body

Connecting with the spiritual body is so important, but it doesn't always take years to do. Use my Power Prayers as a starting point. When you feel shut down and really need a quick connection to your spiritual body, here's a powerful prayer that will help.

God, God, Only God

The following Power Mantra combined with Belly Breathing will immediately put you in touch with your spiritual body, calming you when you feel anxious.

Take a deep breath and place your tongue on the roof of your mouth and say silently to yourself: "God, God, only God," repeating this Power Mantra twenty-one times, and then in sets of twenty-one, until you feel at peace.

Notice that when you place your tongue on the roof of your mouth, it slows down your breathing, allowing you to relax. The energy goes straight to the top of your head, which is your spiritual center. Use the appropriate Power Prayers on a daily basis, and your connection to your spiritual self will get stronger and stronger.

The Field of Love

When you connect to your spiritual body, you merge with a force greater than yourself, a powerful field of energy that I call the Field of Love. This field is the fertile soil in which our love-based desires can grow.

This spectacularly powerful field of energy has many names. Scientists call it the Field of Unlimited Potential; Wayne Dyer calls it the Field of Intention; Deepak Chopra calls it the Field of Unlimited Possibility. You can also think of it as the spiritual realm.

The Field of Love is the force I access to move from the impossible to the possible. I continually draw upon this unlimited creative energy to help me keep up with my two new babies and the demands of my career as an emotional healer and life coach.

Step Two: Connecting the Four Bodies

The Field of Love is magical and capable of creating exactly those things you need to fulfill your desires. Draw it in to you. When you do this, you'll not only feel compelled to make your dreams a reality, you'll have an enormous amount of energy and inspiration to do so. A painter I know says that when she's not in touch with the Field of Love, she can work a maximum of five hours a day before she stops being clearheaded, but when she accesses it, she can paint for ten hours straight without losing focus or her creativity. She says it's as if she has the endorphins of a long-distance runner, and she feels joyful and expansive as the energy infuses every cell in her body, allowing her to double her output.

You can use this spiritual energy any way you want. You might use it to manifest vitality, as I do, making yourself actually start to look younger as you glow from within. You can use it to achieve your dreams. You won't feel that your challenges are insurmountable—you'll just identify with what you want to create, and, if it doesn't work out exactly as you wanted it, you'll simply explore other possibilities because you know something better is coming.

When you draw in the Field of Love using your magnetic power, you'll find you have a feeling of lightness and develop a sense of humor about what used to just stress you out. You'll also find it much easier to be compassionate and forgiving. It's like being in love with a partner who loves you and is there for you: You know that you have a force that's on your side, so it's not so difficult to let things go.

Now, I'm sure the idea of living in a state of love, compassion, and joy sounds pretty good to you, but you will have to work to get there. Use your dynamic energy to clear the toxins and your magnetic energy to heal your physical, emotional, and mental bodies, by using your Life-Shift Tools. The more you access the Field of Love, the more you'll want to keep going back, and the more you'll manifest what you want in life.

Connecting to your Field of Love will help you to turn your

deepest dreams into reality, but there's a wonderful twist. When you do make your dreams come true—and I mean your biggest dream—your physical body takes on a radiant glow, and you are able to access undeniable power. You will laugh and love more easily. You will be able to envelop the loving practices of faith, belief, generosity, acceptance, surrender, gratitude, grace, patience, wisdom, and forgiveness. Through incorporating these spiritual principles into your day-to-day living, you will experience the effect of authentically building your Field of Love as you begin to live your dreams.

These Power Prayers align you with your spiritual body, and allow its energy to flow through you. Say these prayers when you feel you are ready to receive this energy, or if you need to call upon it when you are in a crisis:

+ I deserve to receive the Divine Energy of my higher spiritual self.
+ I feel that Your Divine Energy is working to help me clear the obstacles in my path. Help me create these new possibilities.
+ Thank You for the love and support that You are sending me. I have the trust, faith, and belief in the power of this Divine Love.

5

STEP THREE:
TRANSFORMING OBSTACLES

August 2002, Southern India

It had been two years since my journey to Machu Picchu, and I had done my best to identify and clear the toxic blocks in my physical, emotional, and mental bodies that might have been preventing me from having a child. Yet I still couldn't hold a pregnancy. After three emotionally and physically painful miscarriages, I decided it was time to take my quest to have a baby to the next level. I was about to attempt in vitro fertilization for the first time, and I really wanted to maximize my chances of successfully delivering a child.

My first stop was to visit Siva Baba, a teacher I had studied with for several years in New York. Siva Baba suggested that I journey to India and visit a network of fertility temples where many Indian women make a pilgrimage when they want to have a child. I knew that the unique spiritual energy of the ancient rituals performed at each of these holy sites would act as a strong catalyst for my own quest. Each featured a specific ritual that tapped into the ability to overcome the inner obstacles of fear, doubt, and feelings of not deserving. Actually visiting all of them would surely allow me to break through any energy blocks I was still carrying.

LIFE SHIFT

As luck would have it, my friend Lionel, a doctor and student of Siva Baba's, was planning to go to India to breathe life into a new business he was starting. We decided to go together. Siva Baba outlined a plan for us that involved participating in ceremonies and rituals with certain priests he knew at the temples. Because he was a well-known and highly respected guru, Siva Baba made it possible for Lionel and me to enter ancient temples that were traditionally off-limits to anyone who was not Hindu. I was to become one of the few non-Hindu women to enter this world.

After weeks of planning and organizing, Lionel and I flew to New Delhi and then took another plane to southern India. In the sweltering heat of the holy city of Madurai, I found myself standing in front of the Meenakshi Temple, one of the largest, most magnificent temples in India. It was composed of massive towers 126 feet high, a corridor three-quarters of a mile long (the longest in the world), and huge pillars adorned with twelfth-century sculptures of Indian deities. The energy present in this imposing building was truly awesome and represented the creative power of the universe.

Entering the temple was like taking a step backward in time. Just as the thousands of Hindu women who had been there before me had, I came bearing offerings of flowers and fruits as symbols of my gratitude. I made my way through the throngs of Hindus who lined the immense corridor. Draped in a luminous blue sari, I joined other vibrantly dressed women and made my way toward the inner altar of Shiva, where I was to hand over a list of what I desired. My turn came at last, and I handed my slip of paper to the temple priest. It simply read, "I want a baby." Along with my request, I presented to the priest a beautiful white carnation garland and a coconut, which I was told was a traditional offering because its three indentations are thought to represent the three eyes of Shiva, the god of transformation.

As we traveled from temple to temple, I recognized an underlying feeling of anxiety but couldn't identify where it was coming from. Was it the fear of repeating the past miscarriages, the fear of not being able to conceive, or was it the fear of not having what I want? I knew that I deserved to fulfill my dreams, because I had touched other dreams and desires before. I knew that if I opened myself to the experience, I would be rewarded.

We continued on our journey by traversing the entire country, visiting seventeen temples in one week. Lionel, having been an air force medic, was used to traveling at a highly organized, fast pace. To me, the trip felt like a marathon relay race, jumping on and off airplanes and being met by new guides in different villages. They whisked us away in jeeps, speeding over bumpy roads, dodging cows, driving past long wedding processions and through small villages to take us to our next temple.

One day a guide proudly announced that we were going to visit one of the most sacred temples on our itinerary, Rameswaram (or "water temple"). This temple was associated with the power needed to get rid of one's most stubborn blocks. However, I felt an impending sense of trepidation when I heard the words water temple, as I have a deep fear of parasites. My father had terrified me as a child with stories of his adventures in foreign lands. The inevitable moral of his fascinating tales involved some gruesome disease acquired by his traveling companions who "didn't take precautions" and were infected by any number of parasites. He particularly relished giving descriptions of the flesh-eating variety. My dad had warned me that there were many ways to come in contact with parasites: not only by eating raw foods and drinking the water, but also by bathing, as some parasites can even penetrate the soles of your feet! The only weapon that he trusted as protection was a foul-smelling blue soap that had the acrid aroma of burnt rubber and a foul-tasting array of herbs harvested in the Amazon. Needless to say, he'd loaded up my suitcase with both before I left for India.

When we reached the temple and I looked through its large portal, I was shocked to see both cows and people wading barefoot through muddy, ankle-deep water inside the building. My heart sank as I realized that in all our rushing about, I had left my dad's precious soap back at the hotel, along with my large sack of herbs. My spirits did not improve when the guide began to describe the twenty-one wells from which buckets of water would be poured over us.

True to his adventurous nature, Lionel shed his shoes and waded right into the pool. I didn't know what to do. I had flown halfway around the globe to cover every base on my fertility quest. Was I really going to miss this important ritual because of a fear of microscopic parasites and their flesh-eating diseases? I decided I couldn't take the chance of missing this important opportunity. I took a deep breath, uttered a quick prayer, and shed my shoes, hurrying in after Lionel.

As I rounded a corner, I caught a glimpse of the crowd at the first stone well. Near each well stood a bare-chested priest in a sarong, his arms straining as he hauled large brown buckets of water and dumped them over the heads of those gathered, all the while chanting sacred prayers that would eliminate blocks and cleanse bad karma. When my turn came, I took my place and visualized transformative gold light coursing through my body as the water flowed over me. I said a silent prayer of intention: "I am now willing to release any past or present feelings of disappointment and regret, and any resentments and defeats that I am holding on to in my physical, emotional, and mental bodies. I am willing to go forward with a renewed sense of courage, persistence, trust, and faith, and with a deep sense of gratitude, knowing that a higher source of power is working to support my desire to have a child." I also took heed of my father's warning, tightly shutting my eyes and mouth and plugging my nose and ears with pinkies and thumbs.

I repeated my prayer of intention at each well, and at the end of the day I felt waterlogged but incredibly light. I felt the energy of my spiritual body coursing through me. At that moment, I was connected to my Field of Love. The pain and loss of my miscarriages and the fear that it would happen again were behind me. I walked out of the temple and into the sunlight, full of hope and renewed confidence. I placed my hands on my belly and visualized shimmering silver light coming from the heavens, and I felt the energy of my future babies being drawn to me.

Obstacles Are the Bumps in the Road

Your path to manifesting your desires, dreams, and destiny will not be without obstacles, and while they can slow you down, they don't have to stop you from fulfilling them. I have dedicated my life to helping people not only overcome their obstacles, but actually use them as catalysts. I help my clients see that obstacles are the bumps in the road, fears that need to be transformed. When you have successfully released and transformed them, you are one step closer to your dream.

Our lives are filled with obstacles of all sizes. Some are minute, others traumatic. However, it is important to remember that the magnitude of any obstacle is based on the perception of the person who experiences it. What may be a big problem to one person is only a bump in the road to another. No matter what the size, overcoming any obstacle is part of the process of transformation. When you remove your emotional blocks, the pent-up negative energy is moved and transformed into positive energy. Once you learn how to overcome the smaller obstacles, it will be much easier to hurdle the larger ones.

Many obstacles you will face will seem to be outside of you. You'll think you're blocked from love, marriage, and a family by a man who leaves you, or you'll think your career plans are being thwarted because a job or promotion goes to someone else, or you'll believe that you can't pursue your desires because you don't have enough money. You might think, "It's impossible to get around this, so I might as well give up now." But it's just not the case. When I was in India, the truth really hit home. The fears and limited beliefs you live by are what stop you from asking the big question: "If I didn't think this obstacle was impossible to overcome, what would I do?" When you find the answer to your question, you'll realize that there is no obstacle that can defeat you.

There may have been times in your life when perhaps you experienced a major setback or loss. During these times, you may feel more vulnerable to the paralyzing effect of disappointment and regret, feelings of hopelessness and defeat, and the loss of confidence in yourself and your abilities. No matter how internally strong you may feel, the challenges can seem overwhelming. As you know from your work with the emotional body, if you are holding on to past hurts, resentments, and anger, these feelings are blocking you from using your magnetic and dynamic energies to help you manifest the happiness and joy you deserve.

To get past any obstacle, you need to keep your energy moving so that you can have the strength and resilience to go forward. The key is in first letting go of your fear and anger in order to release the blocked negative energy. With your energy flowing again, you will become more resilient. Know that you are supported by an abundance of universal energy that you can tap into whenever you need it. After using these same techniques, my clients have remarked that they experience a resiliency they never thought was possible. Best of all, they are often amazed at how they were able to turn things around and claim victory over what may have seemed like an impossible situation.

My client Margaret is a perfect example of how an obstacle can be used to manifest bigger dreams. Margaret is a very smart and personable young woman who came to see me because she felt her career in advertising had stalled. One day Margaret was particularly distraught. She told me, "Today I found out that an account I wanted went to someone else. I know the woman who won the account, and she doesn't have a fraction of the creativity I have, and she doesn't do her research like I do. What's worse, she acts like a diva and offends clients, but even so, they always seem to choose her campaigns over mine and then she gets the account. I can't understand it!"

I told Margaret that I knew how frustrating the situation must be. There are some people who seem to have everything come easily to them, and it's not because they have released all their negative blocks and are drawing on the power of their higher spiritual energy. I've had many clients who are extremely successful in their careers despite their negative feelings of low self-esteem, unworthiness, and fear of losing whatever they might have gained. But they never seem to suffer the consequences of renegade behavior and bad choices. Go figure. I call them storybook gods and goddesses.

Some might say these storybook gods and goddesses are just born under a lucky star. The truth is that every person's journey is individual, and it is impossible to compare one person's experience to another's. But what I said to Margaret was, "Maybe your soul has chosen a much more challenging road for you because its goal is to help you evolve spiritually. And maybe your soul places you in circumstances that will encourage you to work through your life's lessons."

I told Margaret that ultimately we are faced with two choices. We can compare ourselves to other people and get bogged down in negative feelings of "poor me," or we can accept that challenges are part of our journey. It's much better to focus on tapping into your spiritual energy and empowering your magnetic and dynamic forces so that you can become stronger within yourself and use your energy to manifest what you desire.

In difficult times, take heart in knowing that every step in your life adventure is important, even the hardships. Each experience brings you closer to allowing your destiny to unfold. Sure, it would be nice if the journey took an easier path. But if that was the case, we wouldn't learn all the lessons we need to learn, so that when we are faced with an obstacle that seems insurmountable, we will be able to harness the energy we need to persevere.

Margaret was broken up, having lost the account she longed for, but she worked with me and used the Life-Shift Tools, particularly luminous yellow light, and the Power Mantra "No one can take away from me what is rightfully mine." She began turning her feelings of resentment and defeatism into creative energy. With this fueling her, she was able to follow her dream and eventually opened her own advertising agency—and it is flourishing.

I can't promise that if you do the exercises in this book and work with the Life-Shift Tools regularly, you will live a carefree, charmed life. What I can promise is that if you use these tools to overcome the obstacles placed in front of your physical, emotional, and mental bodies, you will always be connected to your Field of Love, an energy source that can help you manifest miracles as you pursue your dreams.

Transforming Obstacles into Opportunities

Like the seven deadly sins or the nine circles of hell, there are seven defined obstacles that may be holding you back. Each of these can be transformed into a positive life force energy that you can use to manifest your dreams.

Transform Fear into Courage

In the wake of creating your desires and dreams, your deepest fears may surface, as you are taken out of your financial, emotional, and physical comfort zones. But instead of panicking or freezing, you can learn to use this fear to your advantage. You now have the unique opportunity to shift and transform it into power.

When we are faced with a fear, our natural tendency is to try to deny that it is there. Yet it takes twice as much energy to repress your fears as it does to express them! For whatever amount of fear you experience there's double the amount of power behind it.

Fear is the negative emotional energy that feeds self-doubt, anger, insecurity, anxiety, worry, and general feelings of dread and unhappiness. When you make decisions based on fear instead of desire, you are thrown off your destiny's path and it leaves you in the isolated garden of regret and self-condemnation. You might be affected by fears and emotional toxins that have been weighing you down for years.

There is a wonderful story about two Buddhist monks that illustrates our tendency to cling to negative feelings of fear and judgment.

Early one morning, two monks set off on their way to a distant monastery. Not long into their journey, they came upon a stream that they would have to cross. They walked upstream a short distance and found a narrow and shallow point. Standing there was a beautiful maiden dressed in a simple silk robe. The maiden looked upon the monks with a sad smile and said hello.

"You look sad," said the first monk. "Can we help you?"

The beautiful maiden explained, "I must cross this river, but I cannot swim and I'm afraid."

The first monk said, "Here, let me carry you," and with the maiden's consent, he carefully picked her up and began to wade across the stream, with the second monk by his side. When they reached the other bank, the maiden thanked him, and the two monks continued onward, neither saying a word.

Finally, as the sun was setting, the second monk broke his silence with an angry outburst. "I cannot believe you carried that maiden across the stream! She didn't even ask you for help, and you offered. We have taken a vow not to have contact with any women, and yet you spoke and even touched her body as you carried her across. How *could* you? What will our great teacher say?"

The first monk stopped and looked into the eyes of the second monk. "It's true, I carried a beautiful woman this morning. But I left her on the banks of the stream hours ago. You have been carrying her all day."

When you live with fear, every moment of your life you are faced with a choice: to stay in the fear or to choose to transform your negative thoughts and feelings into positive life-force energy. All of us have moments of fear and self-doubt, even the bravest of us, but you don't have to stay in those feelings or sink further into them. My brother, Curtis Sliwa, is a true testament to courage. On his radio program, he always speaks his mind, even in the face of personal danger. Whether or not you agree with him, he has the courage of his convictions and refuses to be bullied into silence, even though it almost cost him his life.

And my sister, Maria, is one of the most courageous women I know. She is a journalist and human rights activist who spends much of her time exposing the slave trade that even today continues to operate in Sudan, the largest country in Africa. She has risked her life more than once to bring this terrible tragedy to light.

Most of us have had it drilled into our heads from an early age: "Be practical. Think about your future. Don't blow it." It's important to think about things like money and security, but when you let yourself get caught up in the fear of failing or having to become dependent on someone else, you can cripple your ability to manifest your dreams. Howard Hughes was a great example of someone who wasn't afraid to risk everything—every dime he had—to realize his vision. Whether it was creating an airplane that could carry troops and supplies overseas during World War II or making it possible for average citizens to travel the world by plane in safety and comfort, he put all his chips on his vision. If he hadn't gambled and believed in his dream of revolutionizing aviation, think how different our lives might have been.

You may have to risk money, or someone's approval, or risk looking foolish and having people say "I told you so!" But when you achieve your dream, it's the most incredible feeling, and it will all have been worth it. Though I've had many physical obstacles and financial challenges to overcome, finally holding my children in my arms was a triumphant moment in the face of great risk.

Whether your biggest fear is suffering from other people's disapproval, going bankrupt, or being abandoned by those you love, you have the inner strength to overcome these negative thoughts and feelings. You don't have to let deep fears stand in your way. I will help you release these blocks and shift your energy to open yourself up to the extraordinary power of courage.

I use the following exercise with many of my clients, and often did so for myself during my pregnancy. This exercise allows you to face your deep fears and transform them.

Light a blue candle and place it on a stand directly across from you. Sit down in a comfortable position. Take a deep breath, and use your Release Breathing, hold your feelings of fear to the count of five before releasing them.

Place your right hand on your solar plexus as you look into the candle flame and continue breathing. Ask yourself, "What am I afraid of in this situation? What feeling is robbing me of my courage?" Listen to what fears come up from your solar plexus. On the exhale, empty your lungs fully as you blow your fears into the candle light, allowing the flame to consume them.

Afterward, continue breathing. Now that you have released your fears, a feeling of courage will emerge. Repeat the following Power Mantras. If you don't see one that reflects your specific fear, use these samples as a guide to create your own:

+ I am brave.
+ I can find a way to live my dreams.
+ I am more than enough.

The following exercise is similar to the one above but is more challenging because you will dig deeper into your emotional body to release your fears. For this exercise, you will need a fire to sit in front of, or a candle placed in a large pot, as well as your journal and a pen.

Fire Letter

Look into the flame, take a deep breath, then exhale. Use your Connective Breathing and continue this breathing pattern until you feel centered and relaxed.

When you are ready, ask yourself these questions and write the answers in your journal:

What do I fear the most?

What lost opportunities am I having trouble letting go of?

What disappointments and betrayals am I holding on to that are stopping me from engaging in life?

What am I still angry about?

When you are finished, take a deep breath, exhale, and begin to write a letter to the person you are still upset with—and that person may be you! This will help you uncover any other hidden feelings and beliefs you might still have and help you to understand why you created your blocks. For instance, you might write, "Dear Jack, I know that it's been years, but I still feel . . . I'm resentful that you . . . I'm still hurt because . . ."

When you are finished, take your paper and throw it into the fire. If you are using a candle in a pot, be sure to rip the paper into small pieces before feeding them to the flame. As you watch the paper burn, feel the release of all your negative feelings in that empty space; feel your heart open as the unconditional love of your higher spiritual self comes flooding in. It is there to support you to overcome your fears and help you own your courage.

What makes my Life Shift program very effective is that you will always clear your negative energies of fear, insecurity, and limitations before you say the Power Mantra. In this case, if you don't have access to any kind of burning light, you can still do this exercise by using the combination of Organic Breathing and Color Immersion. Choose the appropriate color from the color list and imagine releasing your negative emotions into that color light. Once you have cleared the space, repeat your Power Mantra.

Transform Doubt into the Belief That You Deserve

It's hard to go after a dream if you fear that what you want will never come to you because you don't deserve it, it's too big, or you're afraid you'll lose it. Maybe you think you're just not good enough or talented enough to see your dream fulfilled. But think about all the people who wouldn't have touched your life if they'd succumbed to the fear that they weren't "good enough" to parent you, teach you, help you, inspire you. Where would we as Americans be today if the Founding Fathers had said, "King George is right. Who are we to create a country of our own? Let's just be practical, go home, and get the spring planting done." Or if Thomas Edison had said, "I've failed hundreds of times. Obviously, I just don't have what it takes to make use of electricity. I guess I should just become a farmer."

Many of my clients come to me having been excited about a great idea for a business, a book, a new career, or a possible relationship, only to wake up the next morning with a knot in the pit of their stomach and a little voice saying, "What do I have to offer? What makes my idea so different? Why would anyone want to be with me?" These doubts can stop anyone dead in their tracks! But the first step in counteracting them is to acknowledge that we all have these moments. I've worked with many highly successful people—corporate CEOs, movie stars, and supermodels—whose greatest fear is that someday they'll get "found out," and people will realize that they are not really smart, beautiful, and talented, or that they really don't know what they are doing.

These people feel that it was some cosmic fluke that launched them to such heights, not their own unique talents and gifts. The more successful they become, the more they manifest their dream, the more they are scared of losing it from the fear that they will be exposed. Often they are stuck feeling the inadequacies of childhood, or the wounds of failures and setbacks they may have experienced along the way.

Does this sound familiar? If so, the following exercise will help you release your fears and feelings of self-doubt. The exercise is a major gateway to manifesting your deepest dreams and desires.

That's for Me!

The next time you see something or someone that reminds you of what you'd really like for yourself, I want you to stop and say this Power Mantra: "That's for me!" Whether it's a car or a house, an article of clothing, or a quality someone has, such as confidence or enthusiasm, tell yourself that you can own it. This is an especially good exercise to do if the green-eyed gremlin of jealousy is raising its head or if you feel intimidated by someone. The only reason that you experience envy and intimidation is because you've convinced yourself that you can't have what the other person has—and the truth is, maybe you can.

Identify what it is that they have that you desire, and tell yourself, "That's for me!" Whether you want a healthy, strong body that looks great in a pair of jeans, or a beautiful home, a fabulous relationship, a family, or an exciting career, say, "That's for me!"

The following "That's for me!" Focused Reflection will keep your vibrational rate lifted and keep you resonating with what you desire.

Imagine that what you want is right in front of you, encased in a huge, clear box. It may be an object. It may be you, in a thinner body, having a wonderful relationship, or gripping a suitcase and ready to go somewhere you have always wanted to go. See what it is that you desire. Notice that it is perfectly suited to you, ready for you to own or inhabit. It is simply waiting for you to claim it as yours.

Now look in your hand and see a shiny, sparkling gold key. This is the key to what you desire. It belongs to you. You deserve it.

Walk to the clear box, and put your gold key in the clear keyhole. As you turn your key, see the box become illuminated with brilliant white light and say, "That's for me." Imagine the door swinging open in front of you, allowing you to enter the box. Step inside and claim what you own. Now, walk out of the box, saying, "I deserve this. I own this. That's for me!"

If this exercise is very difficult for you to do, don't worry. As you work through the exercises in this book, come back to this one and repeat it as many times as you need to until you feel comfortable claiming what you desire.

Transform Lack into Gratitude

You will always be faced with a giant obstacle if you are carrying around a feeling of scarcity. When you come from an attitude of lack, you throw your dynamic alpha energy into a tailspin of fear of not having the resources to get the job done. Consequently, you block your magnetic energy from receiving, retaining, and building on what you actually do have. Eric Butterworth, the well-known Unity minister, was fond of saying, "If you have a dollar, say 'Great! I have a dollar!' instead of 'I only have a dollar.' " By expressing "I have" rather than "I don't have," you empower your dynamic energy with enthusiasm to keep going and inspire your magnetic energy to keep opening up to receive. Your vibrational rate lifts, and your energy expands with the attitude of gratitude.

You might be saying, "Aleta, I feel like nothing ever works out for me, so what do I have to feel grateful about?" I know it's not easy when you feel like you are down on your luck. Forget having your cup half full or half empty; you might be feeling like you don't even have a cup! But if you want to change the situation around, you need to vibrate to the higher frequency of "I have" rather than "I don't have," so that you can create the harmonious frequency of manifestation to attract what you desire.

The first step is to acknowledge what you actually do have. Even when everything looks grim, I am sure you can be thankful for something and participate in the following Power Mantra. Think of three things you feel grateful for and say: "Isn't it great that I have . . ."

If you just lost your job and have a family to support, and you don't see another job on the horizon, say: "Isn't it great that I have talents that are valuable and sought after?" Or if you just suffered a loss in a relationship, say "Isn't it great that I have my loved ones around me [or great friends or my pet]?" They don't have to be big things; they can be as simple as "Isn't it great that I have hot water for my shower?" or "Isn't it great that it's a beautiful sunny day?"

These Power Mantras have turned many a challenging situation around for me and rank as a ten on the success chart for many of my clients. Get in the habit of doing this daily, and it will infuse your life with energy.

Each day, I allot time to sing to my children. Their favorite song so far goes "If you're happy and you know it, clap your hands." I sing that song over and over while I am dancing around with them. They are in a totally great mood, giggling and smiling, and I feel exactly the same way. I might not be having a great day, but singing with my twins is a definite energy booster and puts me right into the feeling of gratitude.

My dad told me something I've always carried with me. When he saw spray paint on the wall of a housing project, he said: "The difference between living in a project and living in a mansion is your attitude"—and that is absolutely right.

When you are feeling a sense of lack, transform it into gratitude by closing your eyes and visualizing a burning sun of hot pink while saying these Power Mantras:

- ✦ I am grateful for what I have.
- ✦ More, God! Send me more!
- ✦ All that I need is flowing into my life now.

Transform Regrets into Possibilities

When we feel a door has closed, it can be very difficult to believe that there are other, even better possibilities in our future. It's a natural tendency to want to stand in the hallway, tugging at the doorknob and pounding on the door so that it opens again. Meanwhile, other doors may be opening and we're still stuck thinking about what we lost, stewing in anger and sadness, obsessing over what we could have done differently.

If this is where you are right now, begin the process of life shifting by thinking about these questions:

+ What do I regret not doing that I would never tell anyone about?
+ What do I regret doing that might have hurt another person?

When you acknowledge and let go of your regrets, you will open your energy stores to create all sorts of possibilities that you probably never dreamed of.

If you are still feeling regretful, you can transform the regret into a feeling of endless possibility by visualizing the following Power Mantras written in the royal purple light of abundance.

+ Setbacks happen, but I know I have creative resilience.
+ There's something wonderful out there for me, even though this opportunity didn't work out.
+ Tomorrow will be the best day yet.

Transform Hopelessness into Faith, Trust, and Belief

If you have had the rug pulled out from under you—by divorce, the loss of a job or a relationship, a creative project that didn't come to fruition, or the passing away of a loved one—you might feel disoriented, lost, and emotionally fragile. You may wonder how the universe could let this happen to you. Being in a state of transition is very challenging and emotionally uncomfortable. It's the dreaded unknown that makes us anxious and fearful. Sometimes all you have to hold on to in the absence of any tangible evidence of success is trust, belief, and faith. These beliefs will allow you to carry on. However, during these dark times, you may really feel like you've lost faith, belief, and trust in yourself.

The hardest transitions are when you've suffered a devastating loss or betrayal. Shifting your energy and connecting with your spiritual self is the key to strengthening your faith, trust, and belief that you will be able to create your dreams and rise above your losses. My tool kit is always available to you to help you release the despair during your darkest hours, helping you connect to and receive spiritual energy so you can carry on. I experienced this in a most extraordinary way when I was brought to my knees during one of the biggest betrayals of my life.

A very dear friend of mine had asked me to write a screenplay about his life. I was very excited and honored, and I dove right in. The project consumed me for two years, and I worked endless hours to make it the very best, most honest, and heartfelt rendition of his life that I could. Upon its completion, I bundled up my precious script and took it to someone I knew was well connected to a famous Academy Award–winning director. I waited with nervous anticipation until I got the call from my contact, who told me that the director loved the script. I was thrilled!

I quickly called my friend to tell him the good news. With excitement in his voice, he told me that the director had already contacted him in the hope of negotiating the option for his story. The two of us were elated. Our mutual dream was actually going to come true! It was a time for great celebration, but first I had to fly out to Los Angeles to meet him, the director's agent, and the production company.

I landed at LAX and went straight to my hotel, then called my friend to find out where the meeting was being held. There was no answer. At first I didn't think anything of it, I just waited a bit and then phoned the director's agent's office. His assistant was very friendly and seemed to be aware of who I was and assured me that she would get back to me as soon as she knew any information.

Hours passed and I was still sitting and waiting. As the morning wore into afternoon, I finally heard the phone ring, and when I picked it up and heard my friend nonchalantly chirp, "Hi Aleta!" I got a sinking feeling in my stomach. Something wasn't right. We had been friends for years and had been through so many ups and downs in our lives, but the voice that was coming over the wire seemed unfamiliar. "So . . . how was your flight in?" he said.

I was incredulous at the casualness of his inquiry. I quickly replied, "Fine. Did something happen? I thought we were going to have the meeting at the production company today. . . ."

He hesitated and then said, "Yeah . . . I meant to call you, but you were already in the air."

"Call me about what?" I said, the feeling in the pit of my stomach growing deeper.

"Well, it seems like they want to go with another writer who has worked with the director before."

My mind began to spin. My excitement about having been given the opportunity, and the years of friendship and trust we had built, had drowned out all the warnings my more practical friends had given me—that Hollywood was full of sharks and I should get a signed contract before putting one ounce of creative effort into this project. Instead of heeding their warnings, I laughed and reassured them that the prospect of such a dear friend betraying me was totally ridiculous. How naive I had been! As much as I didn't want to accept it, I knew my golden opportunity had just crumbled to dust.

My friend said in a quiet and concerned voice, "Aleta, are you okay?" The anger and feelings of hopelessness were colliding within me and I couldn't speak. I just hung up the phone and lay on the floor.

I felt as if the wind had been knocked out of me. Time stopped; I must have been on the hotel room floor for hours, for when I finally looked up, darkness had descended upon the city. Inside my heart, I felt a presence, and I knew that I was no longer alone. A radiant white light surged through my body as a voice said, "I am with you." I believe that voice was my higher spiritual body.

A chill ran through me, and a powerful force lifted me up from the floor. As I staggered toward the kitchen to get a glass of water, a wave of calm and inner strength came over me, and I knew I would be okay.

You may be suffering from your own major setback and feel like you can't recover or find the energy to move on. But as I learned through my experience, even plans you think are set in stone can change in an instant. No one knows what the future holds. But if you can stay deeply committed and hold fast to your intention, you can find a way to salvage your dream. Connect to your Field of Love and use that as your energy source. Release your preconceived notions about how your destiny will unfold, and be prepared to embrace the powerful force of your spiritual energy that will guide you through the uncertain waters of transition and change.

When you are feeling hopeless, you can transform it into trust, faith, and belief. Use your combination of Organic Breathing and Color Immersion to help you lift and transform the energy. Then, imagine yourself infused with electric blue light and say these Power Mantras:

- My dream is delayed, not denied.
- Surprise me!
- Hidden forces are working in my favor.
- Good things are coming to me now.
- I have faith that the path to my destiny is being revealed to me.

Transform Defeat into Persistence

I find that the most successful people are not necessarily the ones who are the most brilliant but the ones who are most persistent at overcoming the obstacles to their desires and dreams. As the adage goes, "Perseverance pays."

When I was going through the daunting process of in vitro fertilization, I often watched the movie *Seabiscuit*. It lifted my spirits and reminded me that if I could just keep my faith and carry on, I could come from behind, overcome any obstacles, and cross the finish line to victory. There is a particular scene that I played over and over again. Seabiscuit, trailing behind all the horses, leaps to victory when another jockey pulls his horse back, allowing Seabiscuit to look his horse in the eye. The moment ignited Seabiscuit's passion to win, propelling him to come up from behind and cross the finish line in victory.

What made Seabiscuit's true story so inspiring was that he was at a great disadvantage and was treated badly because of his smaller size and his limited stride. He'd actually been held back and trained to lose races so that other, bigger horses could experience winning. But with a new owner, horse trainer, and jockey urging him on, Seabiscuit ran from his heart, refused to give up, and became a champion. Seabiscuit carried the hopes and dreams of a nation, proving to them that with will, determination, love, and the best support you can overcome the most extraordinary hardships.

I was even more deeply inspired to keep persevering toward my own dream when I read an interview with the author of the book *Seabiscuit*, Laura Hillenbrand. She wrote the book while she was suffering from major bouts of chronic fatigue syndrome and vertigo that made my sciatic pain seem like a mosquito bite. There were days when she was so dizzy and exhausted that she could write only one paragraph. What kept her going was that she identified with the horse and his situation so much that her ability to tell Seabiscuit's extraordinary story was enhanced by her own experience. Writing the book also helped her transcend her physical pain, a true testament to the enormous power of persistence and determination.

When you are feeling defeated, transform this feeling into the energy of perseverance. Use your combination of Organic Breathing and Color Immersion to clear your negative energy and then infuse your intention with indigo light. Write the following Power Mantras on yellow stickies and place them everywhere. Say them aloud every time you see them:

+ I can do this.
+ There is a way.
+ I can and I will persevere against all odds.

Transform Low Self-Esteem into Self-Worth and Confidence

Positive self-esteem is crucial if you want to bring your dreams to fruition. As soon as you begin doubting that you're worthy of the joy you seek, you cut yourself off from receiving it. You can be the smartest, kindest, most creative, and hardworking person, but if you don't acknowledge your own value and you only look outside of yourself for validation, you will get stuck in the realm of the Hungry Ghost. To feel fulfilled, you must start by recognizing that the void is inside of you and that only you can fill it. If you feel that low self-esteem is overwhelming your life and that you are trying to augment your self-worth through excessive spending, eating, or sex, I suggest you put yourself on the Hungry Ghost Diet. This exercise can help you shift from feelings of low self-esteem to being more confident.

The Hungry Ghost Diet:
The Seven-Day Path to Confidence

For seven days try to eliminate any negative statement that deals with lack. For example, refrain from saying, "Nothing is ever going to change," "Great things are happening for everybody but me," "I can't get ahead," "I never get what I want," and so forth.

Every time you make a negative statement, be aware of it and imagine a purple ball of energy in front of you, and as you breathe use your dynamic energy and release the negativity into the sun. Now, visualize what you want to create. If you don't know, ask yourself, "What do I desire?" Use your magnetic energy to connect with your desire. As you draw it to you, feel as if what you desire has already happened. By doing this exercise, you are taking the focus of your energy off of what you don't have and focusing your energy toward manifesting what will truly make you happy.

If you are suffering from low self-esteem, be honest with yourself about your good qualities. Make a list of these and look at it every day. Know what they are, embrace them, celebrate them, and begin building on them. Only you can validate your self-worth. Use your gifts—your intelligence, your common sense, your creativity, your ability to persevere—but use them in the pursuit of *your* desires and dreams, and you will begin to feel better about yourself.

Doing service for others in your community is another way to build up your sense of self-worth. When you are able to give, you are more aware of your talents and gifts, and you feel great that you can do for others. You also connect with people who appreciate you. Search within yourself for what most touches your heart and find a way to give back. It doesn't have to be a big gesture; you would be surprised at the effect of small acts of kindness on both you and the recipient. If you are having trouble finding your purpose, ask the universe to guide you to situations where you can be of help. I know that you have unique gifts that can bring joy and love into this troubled world—you just need to find them and let your light shine.

Transform feelings of low self-esteem into self-worth and confidence. Wrap yourself in an emerald green blanket or visualize an emerald green sun, give yourself a hug, and say these Power Mantras:

+ I am magnificent.
+ I am a miracle.
+ I am divine love.

Energy Bath: Release and Transform

This bath for releasing and transforming emotional and mental toxins was inspired by my trip to the water temple in India. To do it, you will need to either immerse your head under the surface of the water or pour water over your head using a large cup. You will also need to either memorize the prayer that I used in the temple or have it written on an index card so you can recite it aloud while you are in the bath.

As your tub begins to fill, add a few drops of lavender oil to the bath. Take a deep breath in and exhale. Imagine a vibrant turquoise star above your head, and as you begin to inhale, feel its vibrant rays penetrating every cell of your body. Say the prayer: "I am now willing to get in touch with and release any past or present feelings of disappointment and regret, and any resentments and defeats that I am holding on to in my physical, emotional, and mental bodies. I am willing to go forward from today with a renewed sense of courage, persistence, trust, and faith, and with a deep sense of gratitude, knowing that a higher source of power is working to support the fulfillment of my desire." Repeat this Power Prayer several times.

Now, take another deep breath, and as you exhale, release your feelings, thoughts, and tensions as you pour water over your head or immerse yourself under the water. Continue saying your prayer using the turquoise light until you feel a sense of relief and can experience the presence of your higher spiritual self. If you can't feel this connection, just know that it is there and keep releasing your negative feelings into the light, and eventually you will feel the loving presence of your higher spiritual body.

Stay Focused

You can easily slip into putting your dreams on hold by creating new obstacles in your life. Some excuses may be good ones, or you may have important obligations. There is just so much time in the day, and by the end of a busy week you will find that you are no closer to manifesting your dreams than you were the week before. I can teach you the secrets of working with energy, give you practical Life-Shift Tools, and inspire you with stories from my life and the lives of some of my clients who have overcome great obstacles, but if you don't focus and make your dreams a priority, you won't manifest the happiness you desire and deserve.

The key is to remain focused and keep the idea of manifesting your dreams at the top of your priority list. When you are focused, you will plow through any new obstacles in your way and not let them deter you. I want you to make a commitment to yourself today to prioritize your desires and dreams and prune away relationships or commitments that are draining your energy and distracting you from staying on the path. There will be days when this seems like an impossible task and you will get sidetracked, but you just have to go with the flow, release your frustrations, and get back on track tomorrow. If you keep your focus on your priorities, you will be surprised to see how the relationships and circumstances in your life will all work synergistically to help you manifest your dreams.

Some of you might be saying, "Aleta, I'm exhausted just doing what I have to do every day. I can't possibly start pursuing my dreams." Here's the amazing thing I discovered: When you make time to pursue your dream, the energy that you have for "taking care of business" becomes so much greater. When your dream is no longer a distant longing but something real and immediate, it fuels you and makes you feel exhilarated every single time you connect with it.

There are so many ways you can create your dreams by using your dynamic energy:

+ Set aside one night a week to be Dream Night. Mark it on your calendar with a black marker so that you can't break this appointment with yourself and your destiny!
+ Write three desires that connect to the bigger dream on three Post-it notes and place them on your computer or mirror, wherever they'll be in your face. Allow yourself to remove them only when you've followed through.
+ If you have insomnia, stop fighting it and use that hour or so in the middle of the night to pursue your desires: sculpt, read, work out, practice.
+ Let go of your need for perfection. You don't need a spotless house or perfectly manicured nails all the time, nor do you have to be the perfect friend or daughter or employee, available every minute of the day. Delegate chores, give yourself a break on the little things, find shortcuts—do what you have to do to make your priorities the center of your day.

The Temple of Transformation

In the Temple of Transformation, you will energetically shift—you'll dissolve your obstacles and bring in a more positive energy of manifestation. This temple has seven colored chambers, one for transforming each of the obstacles we just discussed: fear, doubt, lack, regret, hopelessness, defeat, and low self-esteem. When you do this exercise, I suggest you work with one obstacle at a time even if you have several of them.

Close your eyes and take a deep breath in, then exhale. Use your Energizing Breathing, which will move your energy out of the everyday world and make you available to your higher spiritual self. Imagine in your mind's eye that you are outside of a temple of shimmering white light. This is your inner Temple of Transformation. Walk forward and enter the temple, taking in the vastness of your surroundings. At the center of the temple is a blazing white flame. The white flame is the essence of all colors, shooting upward into the heavens with all the energies of all the colors combined.

Look around you and notice that there are many chambers, each bathed in the glow of a different color. From your left to your right, see:

+ the vibrant orange Chamber of Courage
+ the bright yellow Chamber of Persistence
+ the emerald green Chamber of Self-Worth
+ the cobalt blue Chamber of Faith and Belief
+ the royal purple Chamber of Possibility and Manifestation
+ the hot pink Chamber of Gratitude
+ the electric violet Chamber of Trust

(cont.)

Knowing the obstacle you need to dissolve, walk toward the chamber of the color you feel drawn to. Enter the chamber and walk toward the flame whose color is lighting the room. Stand there in front of the flame and begin to get in touch with your bodies and the toxins you are holding on to. Ask yourself, "Physical body, where are you holding this dark feeling?" Put your hands on the part of your body where you feel you are holding this emotion—the part where your muscles are tight and you sense agitation. Ask yourself, "Emotional body, what is this feeling?" Is it low self-worth? Fear? Listen to its answer. Continue to breathe in deeply, and exhale. When you are ready, ask yourself, "Mental body, which negative thoughts are coming up?" Breathe in deeply and listen to the response. As you exhale, pull that feeling and thought out of your body and hold it in your hands. Look at it, and see its dark energy.

Hold this ball of darkness in your hand and with great force throw it into the colored fire. Watch as the darkness of the ball dissolves in the brilliant flame. Now see your higher, spiritual body materializing in the flames. Draw it in to yourself, repeating the Power Mantra "I deserve happiness" until you truly believe it. Notice if your spiritual body has reentered you, bringing in the positive energy of courage, possibility, persistence, self-worth, faith, and trust. Feel the transformation within you.

Now walk out of the chamber to the white flame at the center of the temple. Feel your magnetic and dynamic energies in balance, reconnecting you to your dream. Ask yourself, "What do I need to do today to create this dream?" Feel the warmth of the white flame as your spiritual energy revitalizes you. Then say good-bye to the temple and walk out into the light of day and the landscape of your life.

Identifying and transforming your obstacles and bringing in more positive energies is a process, and it won't happen overnight. A life shift is a gradual process, so I hope you'll be patient as you work at getting rid of these obstacles, some of which may be very old and stubborn. After you have cleared the worst of your obstacles, refocus on combining your magnetic and dynamic energies. When you draw on both of these forces, you'll allow yourself to receive support as you seek out and draw to you the people and opportunities that can help you manifest your dreams.

Obstacles challenge you to go beyond your limitations and connect to a higher energy source to resolve them. Emotionally and mentally, we can get thrown off center by our problems and the circumstances surrounding them. We forget that there is a higher source of universal energy that is working for us to manifest our dreams, and through fear and worry we cut off our power to access it.

Don't forget that for every problem you face there is an amazing resource of divine energy that you can tap into that will help shift you to a higher level of benefit. This spiritual source is greater than the fear we are feeling about our limited income, the divorce we are facing, or the health issues that we may be challenged by. When you release and open up the space for this higher energy to come in, this divine power source acts as a catalyst so that you have the power to transform problems and obstacles into positive outcomes.

6

STEP FOUR:
RECEIVING SUPPORT

March 2004, New York City

During my pregnancy, I knew that I was opening myself to criticism from those who didn't understand my intense desire to have children. However, for the most part I was shielded from any negativity. Why was I so protected? Because I believe in surrounding myself with support! My friends, my doctors, my family all understood why I had chosen to get pregnant and respected my decision. That foundation helped immeasurably as I faced the press after the birth of my babies, when some reporters bluntly asked if what I was doing was selfish. Because of the love and acceptance I had received during my pregnancy, some of the toughest questions I faced from the media just rolled right off me.

After all, I'd long since won over my earliest and probably harshest critic: my mother. Like many women, I've had a sometimes tumultuous but always loving relationship with my mother. She is my best friend. However, when I first tried to get pregnant, my mother couldn't understand why I'd want to sacrifice my freedom and compromise my career to have a child. She was also concerned about my age—and hers, for that matter. I know she wishes she could have experienced the twins as a younger grandparent. But in the end, she accepted my dream, and even though she was not in the greatest health, she was always loving and came through for me during my pregnancy.

What ultimately turned my mother around was that she knew that I had another, extended family that would be there for me even after she was gone. She knew I had an extensive support group of wonderful friends. During my pregnancy, I really needed my friends to be there to take the edge off the occasional loneliness I felt and the practical day-to-day challenges that presented themselves. Both during my pregnancy and since the birth, my friends have formed a de facto family around us.

In my work I help other people learn how to attract and receive the support they need to fulfill their dreams. But I was pleasantly surprised when I saw this support manifest in my own life. Because of my independent nature, asking for and receiving support does not always come naturally to me. I also need to remind myself to open up my magnetic energy and allow myself to receive support. Whether asked or not, all the people whom I've helped suddenly showed up to help me. It's as if they were the living embodiment of my healing work.

The ultimate testament to my prayers for support came with the arrival of Edna, my baby nurse. I met Edna about two weeks before I gave birth. I felt an immediate kinship; she seemed like the loving, spiritual person I had prayed would come into my life and help me care for my children. Surrounded by Edna, my family, and my friends, I feel that Francesca and Gian will each have the benefit of brilliant, creative, and supportive mentors.

*T*hose of you who are great at tapping into your dynamic energy know that the hardest thing to do when you're a competent, energetic, independent person is to relax and trust that if you don't do it all yourself, it will still get done. The very thought of receiving support may make you feel uncomfortable and distrustful. But as you may have learned the hard way, not only can you burn yourself out if you block your magnetic ability to receive help, but in many cases, by trying to do everything by yourself, you can actually block the manifestation of your desires and dreams.

So why is it so difficult for us to accept help and depend on others? We may be blocked by the fear of feeling indebted, the false belief that it's better to give than to receive, our need for perfectionism, or just plain distrust. When we let go of these emotional and mental obstacles, our dreams will be embraced by others who know exactly what they need to do to help us out.

Shifting from Feeling Indebted to Embracing Mutual Support

One reason it can be hard to let yourself receive is the fear that you will be indebted to others and expected to "even up the accounts." When you were growing up, you may have been told that nobody gives unless they want something in return. You may feel that you would rather not be put in that vulnerable position of feeling pressured to repay a favor, or you may think that you will not have the resources to give back when the time comes. Even worse, you may fear that the other person will expect you to return the favor by doing something that would compromise your integrity and values.

All of these fears are reasonable in the alpha world. However, we need to draw ourselves back into the Magnetic Feminine. We were created to be receptive beings. When you open yourself to support, you will be surprised by how easy it is to let go of the people who aren't supporting you and to bring in the people who can. For example, a major reason the last painful days of my pregnancy were much easier to get through than they might have been is that my good friend Lisa made the time to come over almost every night and do the dishes, make sure I had enough food for the next day, and fluff up my pillows. She also gave of her talents, drawing on her training as an energy healer to keep me balanced and revitalized. Each time she came over, it felt like someone had just given me a million dollars! Lisa volunteered to help me because she wanted me to realize my dream of having a family. She supported us in the spirit of unselfish service and has never asked for anything in return.

I want you to shift from embracing the concept of indebtedness to embracing the idea of mutual support. In mutual support, everyone gives and everyone receives. You give from the heart with no strings attached, and accept what others have to offer without feeling indebted to them. You support each other out of compassion and empathy. When you embrace mutual support, you feel the freedom to ask for what you need because you aren't afraid that it will come at too high a price. You believe that people, and the universe, are there for you, just as you are for them, when the need dictates. What's more, you end up having enough time and energy to give to others because your needs are being taken care of.

Shifting from False Spirituality to Appreciating the Gifts of Giving *and* Receiving

You may have been told that if you give, give, give and never stop sacrificing, you'll receive your just reward in the afterlife, your next life, or even in this life (eventually, that is!). If you buy into the false spiritual belief that it's better to give than to receive, you end up believing one of two things:

1. You think that if you ask for help, you'll offend the other person just for asking, and that makes you a bad person. This attitude is rooted in the fear of rejection. Be honest with

yourself. Would this other person actually get so angry at you for asking for assistance that they wouldn't want to speak to you again? Would they agree to help you at first, saying "No problem," but secretly be so offended that they'd end up rejecting you altogether? Are these irrational fears, or are you surrounding yourself with people who are unsupportive in the extreme?

2. You think that if you ask for help and the other person agrees to assist you, you're imposing on them, and that makes you a "taker." If you believe that asking others for support is always an imposition, it may be because when you were a child, your parents were always putting their own needs ahead of yours and sending you the message that your needs were a burden. Did you feel you shouldn't ask for attention or comfort because they were overwhelmed with their own problems? This situation is common when one or both parents are self-centered, or if there is another child or family member who requires an enormous amount of attention because he or she is sick or disabled.

If you're afraid that asking for support from someone is an imposition, I want you to embrace a new idea. When you ask for support, you are not taking away from anyone, you are giving others the opportunity to enjoy the gift of giving. One of my clients, Tracy, experienced this when she was given a chance to give back something she had received.

Tracy once told me that she felt very guilty about an experience she'd had. She'd been taken under the wing of an older woman she'd met at her job. She said, "Last year I was going through an awful time, agonizing over whether or not to stay with my boyfriend, because I'd just learned that he was an alcoholic. This lovely woman, Suzanne, was so nurturing and supportive to me. I hardly knew her, but she would listen to me go on and on, and reassured me that I would make the right decision. She never judged me or told me what I ought to do; she just listened and empathized. I ended up breaking up with this man when I was ready to do it, and I joined Al-Anon and started working on my issues. And now I just learned that Suzanne is moving away. I was so busy trying to deal with my life after letting this guy go that I've never repaid her for her kindness. I feel so guilty for having taken up so much of her personal time, unloading my troubles on her."

"Did she ask you to try to make it up to her?" I asked. "Is that why you feel guilty?"

"Well, no, she actually said that I shouldn't worry about trying to return the favor. And I'm going to take her out for a nice dinner before she leaves. But I still feel guilty," explained Tracy.

I told Tracy, "I think Suzanne understands that the opportunity to help other people is a gift in itself. I'll bet she felt great about being able to help you, and you gave her that gift. Whenever you ask for support and allow yourself to receive it, you give another person a chance to feel helpful and needed. And my guess is that Suzanne knows that whether or not you two ever see each other again, the universe will find a way to repay her. And it will give you an opportunity to help someone else. Acts of giving and receiving are all part of the Circle of Giving, which encompasses the great cosmic flow."

I believe in the mutual gifts of giving *and* receiving. When you're having difficulty believing in the Circle of Giving, the following exercise will help you to balance your ability to give with your ability to receive, and let you experience the natural back-and-forth between your dynamic and magnetic energies.

The Circle of Giving and Receiving

Stand up, take a deep breath, close your eyes, and exhale. Inhale slowly and exhale through your mouth, letting go of any tension you feel. As you breathe in, surround yourself with pink light and feel its warm glow gently caressing you.

Imagine yourself encircled by many people—friends, relatives, coworkers, people you know from the neighborhood, even strangers from faraway places. They are all smiling widely, looking at you. You feel their love and gratitude because these are the people you have given to in your past.

Look into the face of the person directly in front of you. Who is she? What gift did you give her? Did you make her laugh when she was feeling sad? Did you give her a ride because her car broke down? Did you help watch her children when she had to work unexpectedly? Remember what you did for her. As she stretches out her arms toward you, feel her appreciation for your gift. Lift up your arms and stretch them out toward her: Place your left hand palm up near your waist, and your right hand near your chest with the palm facing the other person (as if pushing something toward them). Use your dynamic energy and say out loud: "I give this to you" as you send them hot pink light from the fingertips of your right hand. See it enter her body and infuse her with this warm light. This person sends her gratitude back to you in the form of silver light; feel it enter you through your left hand, and feel your magnetic energy drawing it in. Experience this silver light coursing through your body. How does it feel to be supported? What thoughts are coming up for you?

Keep this energy connection, feeling the light flow out of her and back into you, then back into her. Now turn a little to your right and look toward the person standing next to her and extend your hands toward this person. He is smiling widely at you, and you see that his entire body is surrounded by a pink halo. Remember what he did for you. Did he teach you something when you were in school? Did he lend you his cell phone when you were stuck somewhere? Did he offer to make some phone calls and help you find a job?

As you remember each person's gift to you, see the joy in their face as they recall the gift you gave them: the opportunity to help and feel needed. They are stretching out their arms, using their dynamic energy as they send you hot pink light from their fingertips. They say, "Here, accept this light. It is my gift to you."

Say out loud, "I receive your gift." Allow yourself to use your magnetic energy to receive this energy through your left hand. Then use your dynamic energy and send out your gratitude to them through your right hand.

Keep the energy connection to them as you work your way around the circle, remembering the gifts you have given and received. Feel your connection to all of these people and the power of the hot pink light that connects all of you. Thank all of them for their gifts, and for reminding you that when you receive, you give as well.

Now, some of us don't have the problem of giving too much. In fact, you may be blocking yourself from the wonderful experience of giving to others, robbing yourself of the chance to be a part of the Circle of Giving. If you suspect you have this tendency, do the following exercise.

It's All About You

It's truth-telling time! This exercise is for those of you who feel that if you're not the center of attention, you don't exist. I want you to answer these questions very truthfully because maybe you need to learn how to give to others:

1. Do you only ask people how they are so you can jump in and tell them how you are?
2. Are you truly interested in what they're saying, or are you un-interested unless the subject is you?

If the answer to either of these questions is yes, it's time for you to start experiencing the gift of giving and create a give-and-take relationship with the people you love. If you stay self-absorbed, you deny yourself the experience of true connection and intimacy. Make a vow to yourself that, from now on, you will make it a point to listen to the people you care about, be genuinely interested in their every-day lives, and keep track of what is important to them. And if you can't do the work because you are truly not interested in them, maybe this is someone you shouldn't be friends with.

The next time a friend starts talking to you about her own life:

+ Take a deep breath if you feel impatient and want to switch the subject.
+ Count to three before speaking to be sure you don't interrupt. Listen until she's finished.
+ Ask five questions about her life—maybe how she's feeling, how her weekend went, whether she made the decision she was pondering the last time you talked to her, how her children are, and so forth. You may even want to stop and think about what these five topics would be before you pick up the phone to call her, even if what you want to tell her about yourself seems very pressing.

Shift from Perfectionism to Accepting Others' Limitations

Another reason it can be hard for you to receive is that you are plagued with perfectionism: You want the people who can help you to be as reliable and skilled as you are. A lot of my clients who have children experience this need to be in control and have everything perfect, which rears its ugly head whenever they are sick and have to cede their throne of authority to their husband and let him take care of the kids and the house. As my client Kelly said, "It's torturous to stay silent as I watch him dump sugar on the kids' cereal and dress them in clothes that don't match. I know I should be glad the children are being fed and will soon be on their way to school, but it just kills me not to leap out of bed and take charge!"

My reply to Kelly was "Tell me, when your husband takes over for you, what's the worst thing that can happen—really?"

She laughed and said, "Oh, I don't know. Something totally nondisastrous, I guess! But I can't help myself. I have high standards!"

Well, there are times when having high standards, attending to every little detail, and crafting and honing your dream are really important. Michelangelo spent years on his back painting the ceiling of the Sistine Chapel just the way he wanted it to be, and he drove the pope and everyone around him crazy because he insisted on getting it right no matter how long it took. But let's face it—there's a difference between crafting something to be the best it can be and freaking out just because your child is wearing two different-colored socks.

Too often, our perfectionism is rooted in the fear of rejection and inadequacy. When we are in charge of every detail, we feel energized, productive, and in power. No one can reject us, because we're in the driver's seat, and everyone needs us if they're going to get anywhere. I've had clients who were the most overachieving perfectionists in their marriage or their job, and that didn't stop them from being left or fired.

Perfectionism will not ensure that people will stay dependent on you. Like it or not, you have to let go of your need to be in total control if you want your dreams to come true.

Shift from Distrust to Trusting that Support Will Come

You might be saying, "Okay, Aleta, I can relax my standards sometimes. But even so, how do I know I can rely on other people to follow through?" I know it can be very difficult to trust others to help you out when you've been disappointed in the past. The people you counted on may not have come through for you, or they may have done a poor job, not doing what they promised or what you expected. I'll admit that it's always possible that this could happen again if you open yourself up to support. However, if you want to bring your dreams to fruition, you will have to learn to trust again. This will be much easier to do if you attract into your life people you can count on.

One of my clients, Rita, dreamed of starting a community theater group. Rita has always been a mover and shaker, but she recognized that to bring this dream into the light of day, she had to form a team. She opened up her magnetic ability to attract, and not much later, all sorts of people began volunteering time and materials, even low-cost theater space. Rita was jubilant, sharing all the details with me each time she came for a session. But a week before her first production, Rita came to me with a body filled with tension. I could hear the anxiety in her voice as she listed all the troubles she was having with her theater group. "We had a dress rehearsal yesterday, and it was a total disaster. The stage manager had something come up at his day job and couldn't be at the theater, so the fellow who's assisting him had to run everything. The curtain came down before one scene ended, and in the middle of a dramatic moment something crashed backstage. The lead actor stormed off before I could even talk to the cast about the performance, because he was furious at the prop master, who had put his sword in the wrong place. I can't count on any of these people!"

I worked with Rita to release her fears of failure, bringing in the silver light of support, and talked to her about letting go of perfectionism. "Rita, you've drawn in the best, most talented, enthusiastic, and reliable people you could. No one's getting paid, but they're all doing their best. I know because you've shared with me stories about how they've gone above and beyond the call of duty. They share your dream. But no one is perfect. Stuff happens! This is not life or death. Don't lose perspective here. This play is going to come off beautifully. Even if there are some mistakes, you and your theater group are going to move the hearts of the audience. Just keep envisioning this Power Mantra in silver letters on a big theater marquee: 'I always get the help I need to bring my dream to fruition.' "

Rita took a deep breath and promised to see that silver mantra in front of her. The next time I saw her, Rita's face was beaming. "I take it things went well with your show?" I said.

"Well," she admitted, "the assistant stage manager missed some lighting cues, and there was a tense moment when the leading man forgot his lines, but the other actor improvised. Everyone showed up and gave it their all, and the audience went crazy!"

By shifting from distrust to accepting others despite their limitations, Rita was able to keep focused on her dream and enjoy the magical feeling of seeing it come true in front of her eyes.

Are you stuck in the belief that you can't trust *anyone*? Or do you have a fear that if you do, they will fail you utterly? If you have trouble trusting others, remember, your team is only as strong as the weakest link. Open yourself up to drawing in talented and dedicated people to support you. If you have no doubt in your mind that you deserve their assistance, these strong links will start to show up in your life. And when they come, allow yourself to trust them, saying: "My team eagerly supports me."

Learning to Trust Other People and the Universe

We often feel fearful, vulnerable, and weak, unable to trust other people, and as a result we block ourselves from receiving the support we desperately need. The magnetic solution to combating these negative feelings is to remember that you are not alone in the world. You have the ability to draw support from other people and from a source greater than yourself. There are other people who can help you who may have more expertise, or who are more understanding. Even if you have experienced many disappointments and feel that your faith is being tested, continue to do the best that you can, no matter how fruitless it may seem. Eventually, the tide will turn in your favor. Draw upon your magnetic ability to be patient, and let matters take their course.

I used to tell this to one of my clients, Linda, and she would nod and take in my words intellectually, but I know that she still finds it difficult to let herself rely on other people. We were working on releasing her distrust, when she had this lesson driven home very dramatically while whitewater rafting.

Linda was on a trip and fell out of a raft in a very dangerous section of the rapids. In a panic, she immediately clawed at the water, trying to make her way toward dry ground. As she did so, the force of the water pulled her under. With all her strength, she kicked her way to the surface, gasped for air, and started feeling her body bashing against the rocks. "I was terrified," she said, "but all of a sudden, I remembered that the guide had given me instructions on what to do in this exact situation. So I quickly shifted my body into that position, and sure enough, I stayed afloat without getting battered. I just surrendered to the current, trusting that the guide and the team would rescue me just as soon as they could—and, of course, they did."

In a moment of panic, it's easy to forget about all the support that surrounds you and your ability to draw it in. Through prayer and meditation, you can bring in strength, courage, and the answers, people, and opportunities you need. As you start to get rid of your blocks and balance your energies, your magnetic force will be freed up to invent solutions you wouldn't think of otherwise. You'll remember sources of support and start drawing them in.

As I was writing this chapter, the universe decided to provide me with an excellent example of how this is supposed to work! My Internet service went down, my assistant got the flu, and my editor's fax machine broke. Instead of giving in to the fear that I wouldn't be able to get work done, I took a deep breath and let my wonderful magnetic energy do its thing. I called around to my many supportive friends to find someone who could receive an e-mail and fax the text to me, and I trusted that my editor might be able to come up with an alternative as well—and she did. She got a new fax machine. I trusted that when my assistant came back, we'd be able to catch up. I refused to create the obstacles of fear and distrust. I said my Power Mantra "Everything is getting done in perfect timing," and focused on what I had to do to reach my goal.

Exploding Your Obstacles

Whenever you're having difficulty trusting, letting go of control, or receiving support, it's important to check in with your bodies to discover what your obstacles are so that you can blast them away! Are you holding on to fears of disapproval or failure? Is your mental body replaying those old messages about how you can't trust anyone to do the job right? Are you having trouble believing that you are a worthy and generous person, just because right now you're receiving instead of giving? Once you figure out what is blocking you, the following Focused Reflection will help you get rid of your obstacles. After that, it will be easier to let go of your strong need to control situations and start trusting other people to assist you.

Gold Explosion

Take a deep breath in, and exhale. Inhale slowly, and breathe out any tension. Ask yourself, "Why am I having difficulty receiving support?" Now listen for a physical, emotional, and mental response. Is that feeling situated somewhere in your body? If so, place your hands there.

Now picture in your mind a movie screen in front of you and on it project an image that represents what you are feeling—fear of failure, distrust, a sense of low self-esteem. Is it an image of the neighbors gossiping about you? Is someone slamming a door on you as you hold the pieces of an unfinished project in your hand? Do you see a check you gave a friend inscribed with the words *Insufficient funds?*

Inhale slowly, and as you exhale, use your dynamic energy to create a gold sun in your right hand. Feel its force as you throw it toward the movie screen. Watch as the movie screen, filled with negative images, blows up, shattering into thousands of pieces that fall to the floor.

Now, visualize the positive scenario you would like for yourself. Is it a friend laughing with you? Are you holding your completed project in your hands, surrounded by all those who helped you? Is someone you love giving you a precious gift and smiling ear to ear? Inhale slowly, and as you exhale, send forth a beam of golden light from your heart and watch as it circles the picture and infuses it with energy. Hold this image until you feel that it has completely replaced the negative image. Be sure to hold the positive image for at least 33⅓ seconds, because this is the amount of time it takes for your conscious mind to imprint it on your subconscious. In this way, you'll also release your fear and distrust. What's more, you'll be surprised at how you're able to attract people who can support you.

The Dream Team

Of course, it is much easier to trust when you surround yourself with people who are capable of assisting you and who are glad to do it. That's why it's very important to begin assembling a Dream Team of mutual support that will cheer you on, help you out, and give you that extra jolt of energy when you're trying to manifest your dreams.

Building a Dream Team is no small task. It starts with clearing out the closet—letting go of the people who are no longer supporting the changes in your life or who cannot accept your dream. Certain friends who love you "just the way you are" might feel uneasy when you start losing weight and looking very attractive or being more successful. They might feel threatened now that you're "so fabulous." They might begin to act competitive, saying and doing things that make you feel diminished and unimportant. They may even tease you or ridicule your efforts. If these people drain you rather than support you, let them go from your life.

Start building your Dream Team right now by creating a magnetic support journal and doing the following exercise.

Identify Your Dream Team

Inside your magnetic support journal, list the members of your Dream Team and some of the ways in which they've already supported you. Then begin a list of the ways in which you could be supported. For example:

* Use your e-mail address book as a resource Rolodex and share the wealth with the Dream Team.
* Use your Dream Team as a social and professional network.
* Find out what each member of your Dream Team's hidden talents are, and see if these talents are useful to everyone on the team.
* Set up an emergency call list, for backup child care or other times when you need help.

Using this list every day, write down one small way in which you would like to be supported by a member of your Dream Team. Then take a magnetic moment in which you breathe deeply and allow yourself to draw in the support you need. Feel it coming into you. Then start calling your Dream Team and asking them for the specific support you need. Remember, if they can't help you today, they might be able to tomorrow. Or you can call someone else on your Dream Team and ask them to support you today.

Letting Go and Moving On

When the unsupportive person is an old friend, an ex-spouse, or even a family member, separating can be very painful. If you don't feel right cutting off this person completely, or if you can't because circumstances will force you to continue to interact, you can choose to be kind, but keep your distance so that you don't get pulled into the old dynamic. Limit your contact as much as you can and do not engage with this person.

You might find letting go of friendships to be very painful, but if you can remember that these people simply aren't capable of being supportive and positive toward you at this point in their own journey, it will be easier to let them go. It's not your job to change them. Do your best not to personalize their behavior. Consider the source—they may very well be saying or doing something out of their own fears and self-doubt, which has nothing to do with you.

I had a client named Kathy who felt drained and unhappy whenever she interacted with her friend Samantha. I asked her, "Why are you holding on to this friendship?"

Kathy told me, "I've known Samantha since I was four years old and we lived next door to each other. Our mothers are still best friends, and they talk about how wonderful it is that 'we girls' are best friends too. But it's turned into a one-sided relationship. When I was a kid, I was in awe of Samantha—she seemed so smart and invincible and popular. And there used to be a give-and-take to our friendship—she made me laugh and push myself to do things I was afraid to do, like wear makeup or join the math team even though I'd be the only girl on it. But now that I've grown up, I'm just so tired of hearing her go on about herself and her latest drama, whatever it is. She's become an energy vampire!"

"What is your picture of a friendship that you would really like to have?" I asked.

Kathy sighed. "I just want to have fun. I want to hang out and laugh and talk. But I also want to feel heard. I want someone to ask me how it's going with my dream to travel through Europe by bike and actually care when I tell them that I just found someone to stay with when I get to the French countryside. I try telling Samantha things like this, and I can tell she's not really listening, she's playing solitaire on her PC and saying 'That's nice,' like a robot."

Kathy and I worked together to release her guilt and her need for approval from her mother, and Kathy found the strength to end the friendship, dropping out of Samantha's life. "I can't believe how relieved I feel!" she told me afterward. "I was so energized, I called up this woman, Gabrielle, whom I met on a bike trip, and we made a date to go biking together this weekend. She's such a lighthearted person. I really enjoy just biking around with her and chatting. She was so impressed with my plan to bike through Europe—she wanted to hear all about it!"

Kathy and Gabrielle developed what I call shared energy. Their relationship was built on mutual support. Neither was acting self-centered, so each could benefit from the other. Consequently, they were each receiving some of the other person's energy. Their shared energy continually fed off each other, and in turn elevated the relationship.

Closing Your Circle of Energy

The next time you are with a person who drains your energy, use your Relaxation Breathing and make circles with your hands by placing each thumb against the middle finger of the same hand. You can do this discreetly, keeping your hands in your lap or underneath a table. This is a yoga position that actually creates a circle of energy, containing your energy within you so that it can't be drawn from you.

Now, notice whether this person, who usually takes energy from you, cuts off the conversation because you are not feeding his or her energy.

Letting go of unsupportive people is like cleaning out your closets. It's difficult to part with your prom dress, but it doesn't fit anymore, and you really have to clear out the old to make space for the new. When you have friends who aren't supporting your dreams or making you happy, you need to let go of them and create the space to let new people come into your life. Trust me: There will be plenty of new, supportive friends to replace the old ones. You're going to attract them using your magnetic energy. If you're having trouble deciding whether or not to let go of certain people in your life, ask yourself the following questions. Again, consider writing out the answers in your magnetic support journal:

1. Does this person listen to your problems without judgment, and then offer loving support and genuinely constructive advice, saying, "If it were me, I would . . ." instead of "You really should . . ."?

2. Are they always creating some kind of drama and expecting you to come tearing in to rescue them?

3. Does this person genuinely share your joy over your successes and encourage you to go further, without offering left-handed compliments like "Wow, you did it! It's just so hard for me to believe, because, you know, you've always been so unfocused."

4. Are they appreciative when you do kind things for them, or do they take your help for granted, always wanting more?

5. Does this person do nice, thoughtful things for you?

6. When you are around them, do you feel good and energized, or do you feel drained?

7. Does this person aspire to manifest their desires, dreams, and destiny? Do they genuinely want the same for you?

8. Can they forgive you after you've done something that upset them?

9. Are they understanding and loyal, sharing your values and integrity?

10. Is this person competing with you in your personal life, your professional life, or for another's attention? Is this competition healthy or vindictive?

If any of these people show signs of selfishness or lack of support, ask yourself if this is what you have come to define as friendship. If you don't like what you see, then let them go—now. You don't need to waste any more time or energy. My Releasing to the Heavens exercise will help you let go of these burdensome people and entrust them to the care of a higher power.

Releasing to the Heavens

Buy an orange helium balloon, and shortly before dusk, as the sun begins to set, face west. Breathe slowly and deeply as you remember the joy that you previously experienced with this person. As the sun sinks into the sky, its last rays reaching upward from the horizon, say, "I cherish our past relationship, but I no longer have the need for negative relationships in my life. I release you to your highest good." Let go of the balloon. Watch it float upward to the heavens and say, "My magnetic energy only attracts high-vibration, supportive people."

Assembling Your Dream Team

Now that you have released from your life all the people who cannot support you, it's time to tap into that wonderful dynamic energy of yours and start meeting new people. You may already have many supportive people in your life, like the ones you listed earlier in your magnetic journal. As you begin to put energy into your desires and dreams, start thinking about adding some valuable team players. Here's a list to get you thinking about the supportive people you might want to draw into your life and put on your Dream Team. In fact, try to find some backup people for each position in case your primary person is unavailable.

1. Who are the people in your life whom you feel really safe with—safe enough to confess your darkest feelings and deepest secrets to, knowing that they will accept you and never betray your trust?

2. Whom can you trust to help you out in an emergency, someone who can drop everything and lend you practical and emotional support?

3. Who can mentor you and give you encouragement as well as really great objective advice about achieving your dream?

4. Do you have peers who are in a similar situation who can empathize with you and encourage you?

5. Who can remind you of the importance of balancing your everyday obligations with your need to pursue your dream?

6. What sorts of professional people can help you stay as healthy as possible?

7. Whom can you rely on to give you comfort and emotional support when you're struggling?

8. Do you have someone who won't mince words and will tell you exactly what you need to hear even if you're uncomfortable hearing it?

If you don't have these positions on your Dream Team filled, you've got to go out there and start meeting new people! Be proactive. If you want people to show up, you can't hide under your bed hoping they'll read your mind, call you, and offer to help. You've got to let them know what your intent is and how you want them to support you in making your vision a reality. Trust me, there are many energizing people out there who are fully engaged in life, who can bring their enthusiasm, support, and creativity into yours.

I know that it is difficult for many of you to put yourself out there, but try to imagine that you're a curious child, uninhibited about talking to strangers. No one's going to bite your head off or turn their back on you because you engaged them in a conversation! Release those fears of rejection and get out there and say hello. You may be surprised at just how quickly you're able to draw wonderful new friends and supportive people into your life.

My clients often share with me marvelous stories about how, once they stopped blocking their magnetic energy to attract while using their dynamic to go out and meet people, the most astonishing things happened. One client, Lila, dreamed of being a novelist, but for years hadn't breathed a word about it to anyone. She began sharing her aspirations with other people at church and in her neighborhood, and one day she met a woman in the park who told her, "My sister is a literary agent, and your novel sounds just like the type she's always looking for. I'll give you her number!" Another client, Amanda, longed to run a bed-and-breakfast. She kept imagining herself surrounded by a warm blanket made of silver light as she repeated her Power Mantra "The bed-and-breakfast is looking for me." After months of drawing on her magnetic energy and sharing her dream with people, she learned that her new boyfriend's cousin had a bed-and-breakfast and needed help running it. Amanda met the woman, they hit it off from the moment they met, and now they successfully run the bed-and-breakfast together.

When you shift your energy and stay focused on manifesting your desires and dreams, the universe responds in unexpected ways.

The Chat Room of Discontent

As you draw in new people, be sure that they're supportive in a positive way. Women often form negative support groups—what I call the Chat Room of Discontent.

We all need friends to listen to our hurts, angers, and frustrations. There's tremendous comfort in knowing we can be honest about our not-so-pleasant realities and still be accepted by people who love us. It's healthy and natural to bond with other women who will support us as we express our darker feelings of sadness, hurt, and anger. This type of sharing allows us to release those feelings and shift our energies to envision a better situation and to make positive changes.

But in the Chat Room of Discontent, our girlfriends encourage us to vent our frustrations but not to let go of them. When we complain, they respond with, "I know, men are such jerks. Every last one of them!" and "Isn't she annoying? And there's nothing you can do about it. You just have to put up with her."

When women get together and let their dark feelings resonate to each other's negativity, they cause their magnetic energy to keep attracting the same self-defeating outcomes. When yet another man turns out to be a cheat, or another fabulous opportunity turns out to be not so great after all, the Chat Room of Discontent breaks into the old negative Power Mantras of "I told you so, you can't win," "Men can't commit," "Good girls finish last."

If you're feeling unhappy and unappreciated in a relationship, it's good to have a friend who can validate your feelings and gently nudge you to look at all your options about the situation while reminding you that you deserve to have your needs fulfilled and to feel cherished. In fact, if you need help changing a situation that is draining you and making you miserable, an energy healer or a therapist, who can be objective, may be able to help you in a way your friends can't. It can be very difficult for people who love you to step back when they see you in pain and give you the room to make decisions in your own way and in your own time.

When you see that your friendships are helping reinforce your disappointments, resentments, and fears, it's time for you to shift from complaining to problem solving and offering your friends positive support. Tell your friends that you'd like to change the energy of your conversations and make them more productive. When they vent, don't express your empathy by topping their story with another one that's even more depressing. Simply say, "I feel for you. That's a tough one. I'm sure you'll figure it out. Let me know if you want my help working this through." And change the subject if you have to.

As we get older, it's easy to slip into the Chat Room of Discontent whenever the subject turns to our health. Suddenly, everyone's comparing aches and pains and complaining about doctors and HMOs. Wouldn't it be more revitalizing to talk about a great new healthy recipe you learned or a fun opportunity for exercise that you just discovered? Feed the positivity, and resonate to each other's higher vibration.

Giving Too Much

When the people close to you are not supporting you in your desire to stay in a positive state of being, you may be tempted to just keep pouring your own positivity into their well, hoping to fill them up so that someday they will dip into their well of resources and give back to you. You may buy into the philosophy of metaphysics that states: "If you want something from someone, give it to them." This works very well for people who tend to be self-centered and self-absorbed. However, if you're the type who sacrifices for others at the expense of your own well-being, thinking this way will just send you into burnout as you turn into Lady Bountiful, constantly giving.

Do you need to wean yourself from somebody you've been giving too much to and free up your energy to draw to you what you desire? If so, you need to pull in the energy cord that reaches from your solar plexus out to the people you are siphoning off energy to. The following Focused Reflection will help you disconnect.

Pulling in the Energy Cord

Sit in a comfortable place, close your eyes, and start your Energizing Breathing. Visualize a cord that reaches out from your solar plexus into the solar plexus of the person you feel is draining you. Ask yourself, "Why am I connected to this person? What was it that originally attracted me to the friendship? Is this person holding up their end of the relationship?" If you hear yourself give negative answers, you need to end your energy connection to them.

Inhale, and then deeply exhale. Ask yourself, "How can I disconnect this cord?" Do you need to yank it toward you, detaching it? Do you need to burn it or cut it with a knife? Do what you have to do to break the connection and feel a sense of relief as you see the cord break. Now, draw it back into you and feel it coil up inside your solar plexus. Inhale, and as you exhale, bless the person you have disconnected from, saying "I release you in love and light."

A Variety of Supporters

Too often, I see women putting far too much pressure on their primary relationships with their husbands, best girlfriends, or mothers, expecting them to be everything to them. It's wonderful to have a variety of people on your Dream Team, and to have a lot of them. For instance, I have several friends who are healers or therapists whom I call when I need to shift my energy. I also have several people who have amazing Rolodexes and can always connect me to someone who has information that will help me. And I have people who are happy to come over and babysit. If someone is unavailable, I'm not stuck, because there's someone else who can help me out. Sometimes the person who can help you one day can't help you the next because of their own obligations. If they can't come to my aid when I need them, I just release that to the universe, knowing that the right person will be there for me.

You may decide to keep your whole Dream Team in the dark about something because you feel it will dissipate your energy to tell a lot of people about your desires until you've gotten them solidified into a dream. When you're ready, you'll speak up, knowing they are there for you. Then, too, you might want a certain amount of privacy. Many women don't let anyone know that they're pregnant right away because if they miscarry, they want to be able to decide whether or not to tell people. But as soon as I was pregnant, I told several people right away because I knew these particular people would send prayers and be supportive to me.

You Will Never Be Alone

When you open yourself to support, you will find that people are attracted to your dreams. If you felt alone in the world before, you must have been blocking your Magnetic Feminine energy. Once it is running again, you will find that you can attract all sorts of supporters. But don't let your fear of being alone force you to make bad choices. Choose your new friends carefully, and they will be with you for a lifetime. What's more, they will embrace your dream and help you manifest its reality.

7

DREAMING OF LOVE
AND ROMANCE

November 12, 1947, Chicago

From the moment I entered the world, I was very much shaped by the first love of my life: my father, Chester. As a young girl, I adored him. I can still remember the excitement of coming home from school and seeing his sea bags in the hallway, signaling that he was back home. My mother treated each return like a hero's homecoming. The return of a hero. When he was home, he'd regale the family with amazing tales from around the world. My dad is a great philosopher; he usually reads a book a day. Even now, my siblings and I call my father whenever we have a question about anything, because we know he'll have the answer. He's like our family's own Ask Jeeves.

Whenever my dad was on a voyage, my mother was the glue that held everything together at home, and my brother, Curtis, and sister, Maria, and I all supported her and one another. It was always sad when Dad had to go back to sea, but I always knew he was there for me in spirit, and seemed to miraculously arrive home when we needed him the most.

My relationship with him forged an independence in me that has been a bit of a double-edged sword. I love men and I've had wonderful relation-

ships with some great ones. But I also have a side of me that is a bit of a free spirit, someone who needs to be "alone at sea" every now and then.

My parents have a great marriage. They are independent spirits who are upbeat and capable alone or as a pair. Growing up in this environment, it never occurred to me that relationships could be otherwise. But as I matured, I realized that there are many different types of men and women. I became a woman who never allowed a man to control me.

I was once in love with a man named James, a strikingly handsome, charismatic artist whom I met in my late twenties. We had an exciting, passionate relationship, but our strong personalities sometimes clashed. When I was twenty-seven years old, I wanted to go away to meditate in a Tibetan-style hermitage in the woods of upstate New York for several weeks. Even though James was open-minded about my spiritual work, he thought that weeks in the woods sounded crazy. He thought that if I wanted to be away from him for so long, it must be because I was having an affair.

I couldn't believe he was making me choose between him and the possibility of attaining spiritual enlightenment! I knew he'd end our relationship if I went on the retreat, but I felt I had to follow my spiritual path. Ultimately, I chose the woods over James, but even so, don't think I didn't suffer. Every morning for a year after the breakup, I woke up with a knot in the pit of my stomach, still missing him terribly.

I've had five great loves in my life, and I am so thankful to each of them. The men I fell in love with were as eccentric and iconoclastic as I am. None of them were typical husband or father material. Yet I learned so much from each of them, especially when our time together came to an end. My greatest love died a few years ago, and his passing really emphasized my desire to have children.

I fully intend to have a next great love. Because of Francesca and Gian, I hope he'll be my last. Today I'm looking at what I need in a different way. And because of what I learned from my past loves, especially the gifts of forgiveness, compassion, and letting go, I am looking forward to what the next man will bring into our lives.

It All Starts with You

We all want to love and be loved. For many of us, our deepest dream is to find a life partner who will support us emotionally, mentally, spiritually, and, dare I say it, financially. We grew up with the same fairy tales, and we expected those same love stories to happen for ourselves. We thought that our perfect soul mate was just around the mountain bend, and that he'd come and literally sweep us off our feet, bringing with him everything we could possibly want.

Now, this would be a convenient package, but unfortunately I haven't yet met this fabulous man, and neither have any of my clients, nor my women friends. Granted, there are some amazing men who are supportive, sensitive, who really try to be communicative, and who have the capacity to be emotionally connected and available. But unless you are the most accepting woman on earth, each relationship develops its own particular challenges. It can be a financial one, a crazy ex-wife, difficult children, health issues, or work issues. It's always something.

Yet the fantasy persists because it is fiction, and it's an easy way to wrap up a story. But we do not live in the world of fairies, and there is hardly a princess among us left to save. In the real world, we have to find our princes on our own. But don't fret. Real, loving relationships do happen every day, and there is someone out there ready to love you and be loved in return. I can't promise you Prince Charming and a happily-ever-after ending, but I can promise that by using my Life-Shift Tools you will awaken that male magnet in you. Once you've connected to it, you will learn how to keep a loving relationship growing and getting better.

Many of you may feel like I did, that by a certain time in your life you should have everything in place—relationship, career, and family. But more often than not, the universe doesn't obey our time schedules! When you start believing you've got to find "the one" by the time you're thirty, or by the end of this year, you may start making bad relationship choices based solely on fear. I want you to make good choices based on your deepest desires and on what will bring you true happiness. Those clients of mine who have rushed into relationships because they were lonely and scared all lament that there's nothing lonelier than being in a bad relationship.

While we tend to blame "outside forces," such as other people or situations or careers, for wreaking havoc on our romances, the real obstacles are inside of us. Unknowingly, you can be stopping yourself from attracting the relationship you desire and dream of. So, and I'll say it again, the first step to fulfilling your dream always begins with you. The more you can truly love yourself, the more you can love others and receive the love they have to give.

The Greatest Love of All

The only security any of us has, and the only thing we can always control, is how we feel about ourselves. Men can come and go, great loves can fizzle, or, sadly, we may be left alone following a divorce or death. The only security of love that we can control is the love that we have for ourselves, which is ultimately the foundation of true happiness.

You might be saying, "Aleta, I've heard this all before. Love myself? What does that really mean?" I know it's hard to understand, and love means something different to everyone. But loving yourself is not an intellectual exercise that occurs in the mental body. It's an experiential shift that needs to include your emotional, physical, and spiritual bodies as well. When you get all your bodies in alignment, harmonizing with one another, and your dynamic and magnetic energies are engaged, you will truly experience what it is like to love yourself.

Dreaming of Love and Romance

In my practice, I use the power of self-love to help women connect to the positive energy of who they truly are. For many of you, loving yourself may be difficult at first. Have no fear, I will help you uncover past experiences that may be blocking you from loving yourself and from attracting and having a great relationship. If in your childhood you did not form a strong sense of self-worth and confidence, it will take time and work to develop it now. You will have to unlearn some of the messages from your early years that may have been planted by those who were supposed to be your allies, including your family. But it can be done! Some of the most magnificent women alive today have triumphed over extreme challenges in their childhood. These are women who have worked hard at healing themselves internally, and as a result, they've been able not only to achieve their dreams of a career, but to draw in men who are loving and supportive, and right for them.

When you begin to truly love and accept yourself, you can approach your relationships from a point of wholeness and self-confidence. Feeling complete within yourself, you will want to share your life with another person. And if it doesn't work out, you won't be permanently devastated, because you will still have a powerful relationship with yourself, and the ability to manifest something even greater in your life.

When Laura first came to me, she was thirty pounds overweight and very dissatisfied with the cards life had dealt her. She was an extremely talented and successful floral designer whose work phone was ringing off the hook, yet her private line was always quiet. After years of working eighty-hour weeks and having no time for a personal life, she became depressed. She didn't want to give up this great business opportunity, but emotionally she felt gypped. The one thing that she desperately wanted, from the time that she was very young, was to find her true love and have a family, and that childhood dream seemed to be taking a backseat to her career.

Overwhelmed by her responsibilities, she said to me, "I feel like my career is taking away any chance of ever being with a man, getting married, and having a family."

I told her, "Having love or having a career is not an either/or choice. You can have both, and you don't have to hide behind one when you don't have the other. Don't use your job as an excuse for not having a relationship. Instead, we can work on releasing your insecurities so that you can love yourself. Then you'll be able to believe that you can have both a career and a relationship. But more important, you will believe that you deserve to have both by releasing the belief that in order to be successful you have to sacrifice your personal needs because of your business demands."

Laura was not happy about my suggestion that she focus on herself instead of on finding a man to fit into her life. I practically had to drag her kicking and screaming into working on releasing her deep feelings of low self-worth and distrust of others, and overcoming her belief that her career was "the enemy." Eventually she realized that as much as she desired a relationship, deep down she felt that she was unlovable, and that her feelings of mistrust and fear of abandonment were causing her to push available men away. I helped Laura release her emotional blocks of anger and hurt and her mental blocks of low self-worth through breathing and releasing exercises to connect her to feelings of inner love. In time, she was able to tap into her magnetic energy to attract into her life a man who was totally perfect for her, who was available, who adored and cherished her, and this new man especially loved that she was a successful career woman. There were times when she had openings that she needed to work around the clock to install or he had to go away on business trips for weeks at a time, but they made a pact that they would make their relationship the priority and see each other at least twice a week when he was in town, even if it was just for dinner so that they could stay connected and build their love.

Letting Your Spiritual Body Support You

One of the most important pieces of my Life Shift program lies in achieving self-love through accessing your spiritual body. Your spiritual body is pure light, and it loves you unconditionally, steadily, and reliably. This spiritual force is always there for you, ready to pour down its loving energy into you, no matter what happens. It has no judgment: It can show you life's different possibilities without trying to control which ones you choose. It knows that whatever choice you make will take you down a certain path. Some choices will make your path bumpier than others, but your spiritual body will ultimately lead you to your dreams—and to the relationship that will enrich and fulfill you.

The direct path to experiencing the love your spiritual body has for you is to be gentle with yourself. What blocks your connection with your spiritual body is your self-criticism. You probably don't realize just how much energy you spend tearing yourself down instead of building yourself up. When you repress your feelings, you actually use up your energy stores, leaving you with little left to develop a loving relationship. What's more, the energy you will have will not be a good representation of your spiritual self. A partner will mirror back how you treat yourself. Because this energy is surrounded by your own fears and insecurities, it can only attract a partner whose inner life reflects your own. You might feel hurt by his criticism and lack of appreciation and support, but you need to look at how you are criticizing and not appreciating and supporting yourself. Once you eradicate that pattern, you will experience a total shift in how your partner treats you, and the types of partners you will be able to attract.

I once asked a client what she thought the payoff would be if she could stop herself from self-criticizing. Her answer was that eventually she would change. I had her make a list of all the things she wanted her husband and friends to say to her that showed their appreciation and then repeated that list back to her. Once she started believing in the words on the list, she began to believe in herself. She was amazed at how her husband became less critical and she began receiving lots of appreciation and compliments all around. While other people's behavior might have changed, the true life shift occurred when she became more self-confident, so that she didn't take others' comments as seriously. This client had a mental shift in the way she perceived herself, and by doing so was able to free up her energy and connect with her Field of Love. At the same time, when you are treating yourself with love, the flow of love and support from your spiritual body will be vibrating at a higher level. You will be able to draw to you and receive the love and support you deserve.

When you acknowledge that your spiritual body is there and open, your physical, emotional, and mental bodies will be able to receive its love. However, there may be times when you feel like every aspect of your life is under siege and destabilized no matter how much you work to release your fears and angers. You might find it hard to sleep or you wake up with feelings of anxiety about the successful outcome of situations. You feel worn down by having to deal with one challenging situation after the other. You find out that your health insurance just got canceled right before you are facing a major operation or you get a letter telling you that your daughter's tuition is going to double the following year. You find a receipt for lingerie in your husband's coat pocket and you know it wasn't for you. You feel so unhinged that you can't seem to find your trust and faith in your spiritual power. *Know* that there is a greater power working through all the chaos for your highest good.

The following is a great Focused Reflection for you to experience the power of your spiritual body coming to support you.

Opening to the Spiritual Body

Lie down, and breathe in deeply, using the Belly Breathing technique. As you breathe, let yourself become aware of your four bodies, the Russian nesting dolls inside of you: your physical body, surrounded by your emotional body, surrounded by your mental body, all three of these bodies housed within the largest nesting doll, which is your spiritual body.

Exhale forcefully, releasing any toxins these bodies may be holding on to. Feel your spiritual body pulsating with luminous white light and beaming it inward to your physical center, your tailbone. Feel your tailbone fill with this light energy. Focus on feeling a reciprocal flow of love and appreciation from your spiritual body to your physical body. Then breathe this luminous white light into your heart center. Feel your heart center fill with this loving light energy; begin to feel a reciprocal flow of love and appreciation from your spiritual body to your emotional body. Now breathe this luminous white light into your third eye, the spot in the center of your forehead that serves as the gateway to your spiritual intuition. Feel your whole head fill with this loving light energy. Begin to feel a reciprocal flow of love and appreciation from your spiritual body to your mental body. If during this process, you find that one or more of your bodies is feeling a resistance to receiving the love and support from your spiritual body, ask yourself why. You might feel like you don't deserve this connection. If so, release all negative feelings into the white light and watch them burn up. Once you have released any negative feelings, feel the power of unconditional acceptance as your spiritual body's light rushes in, infusing each of your bodies with love. Float in the support of this unconditional love, as if you were floating on water. When you are ready, open your eyes.

Transforming Hurts of the Past

If you are unable to forgive someone—another person or your-self—or if you fear abandonment or have low self-worth, acknowl-edging and healing through releasing old hurts and wounds with low-vibration energies will open you up to receiving the higher vi-brations of love.

I know that when you've been hurt, it can be extremely difficult to heal. But hanging on to resentments will tie up your energy. This happens because the energy in your cells is stuck in a constant replay of this bad memory or bad feeling about yourself or others. Remem-ber my client Joan, who kept punishing her husband, Tom, for his past behavior of speaking harshly and sarcastically toward her? By putting up her defenses, continually punishing him, and refusing to forgive him, she blocked herself from receiving his love and ulti-mately wound up punishing herself. The reality is that when you set up a wall to keep out pain, you also keep out love. Forgiveness is cru-cial for your well-being. When you release the emotional energy of anger and hurt, you are freed up to learn from your experiences and go on to create the happiness you desire. The reason you forgive someone is not to let them off the hook, but to free your energy so that you are not constantly vibrating to the memory of your past hurts. Then you can go on to rebuild and create something far more fabulous in your life. This was especially hard to do for my client Pamela, who suffered from a trauma that she was having difficulty getting past. Pamela came to me shortly after filing for divorce. Her husband, Russ, was a talented visual artist who never made much money, and, unfortunately, developed a drug addiction that caused him to lose job after job. When Russ first went into rehab, three years into the marriage, Pamela stuck by him. He did kick his habit—for a while. A few months later she found drugs in his coat pocket again and felt betrayed. Pamela vowed to leave him then and there, but

Russ, his family, and their counselors pleaded with her to give him another chance. Pamela caved in and stayed.

After the fifth time he entered rehab, Pamela had had enough. She was exhausted and ready to put the past behind her. But to her shock and dismay, her divorce became a bitter contest over their personal belongings, including the apartment she had bought with her own money, the pension fund she'd built up, and all the cash she'd accumulated through her hard work. As the divorce proceedings went on, it became clear that she was going to be forced to buy Russ out of their marriage. Understandably, Pamela's first reaction was to become furious with herself. "How could I be so stupid? I stayed because I felt sorry for him, and then, because I hung in there for twelve years, he was legally entitled to half of what I have. As far as I'm concerned, I never want to be in another relationship again."

I asked her, "If there was a guarantee that a wonderful man who really loved and supported you would come into your life, would you feel the same way?"

She thought for a moment and said, "Well . . . no."

I explained to Pamela that although she was entitled to feel angry and resentful, she was also entitled to that wonderful relationship she dreamed of—but she wasn't going to get it if she blocked herself with resentments and regrets. "Let's work on the assumption that the loving, supportive man you long for is out there. You need to forgive Russ for *your* sake, because your lack of forgiveness is tying up your energy. Yes, you're going to keep out any other man who might use you, but you're also going to keep out the man you long for, the one who will cherish and love you."

I wanted Pamela to get in touch with the power of her creative resilience, that ability to bounce back from hard times and manifest new opportunities. She also worked with the healing power of royal purple, the color of abundance and forgiveness. With much effort, over time, Pamela was able to forgive Russ and herself, and she is now dating a man who is extraordinarily loving. He is 100 percent connected to her and gives Pamela the love and the emotional and financial support that she deserves.

Whenever you are having trouble forgiving yourself or someone else for events that happened in the past, know that there is a higher spiritual force that is working in your favor, looking out for your highest good. Take back your power from that other person—release the idea that the support and love you need must come only from them and open yourself to receive the love and support of others.

Release and Forgive

Take a deep breath in, and exhale; begin using your Relaxation Breathing technique. Imagine a gold chalice above you filled with liquid silver light. Then tip the chalice over, pouring down its liquid silver light into your body as you take a deep breath and place your hands on your heart. Ask your emotional body, "What did this person do that feels unforgivable?" Did they lie to you? Spend all your money? Betray you? Now ask, Did you trust him or her even though you sensed you shouldn't? Did you stay with this person too long? Did you lie to yourself about the way you were treated and make excuses for their behavior?

What emotions are you holding on to? Anger? Resentment? Shame? Regret? Find the place in your physical body where you are holding that emotion. Place your hand there.

As you inhale, surround these emotions with silver light, and as you exhale, feel those negative feelings dislodging themselves and being absorbed by the power of the light. Then, ask your mental body, What beliefs are you holding on to? That men can't be trusted? That you're foolish? That you're a poor judge of character? That no one will ever love you? Where are these feelings lodged in your body? Place your hands there. Breathe into those thoughts, and as you exhale feel them being drawn out of your body and absorbed into the liquid light.

Now place your hands on any area of your body that may be injured or have a health issue. As you inhale, surround that area with the magnetic silver light and ask your body what feelings are lodged there. Be aware if they are similar to what you were thinking and feeling in your mental and emotional bodies. Holding on to these feelings can create your physical problems. Tell these pains that they are no longer serving you to get well, and then exhale. Let whatever comes up be absorbed by the magnetic power of the silver light.

As you increase the vibrational rate of your three bodies by clearing out negative thoughts and emotions, you will automatically connect to the higher vibration of your spiritual body. Feel the sense of expansion as your bodies begin to harmonize with one another.

As a space opens up inside of you, feel your spiritual body healing your past wounds, hurts, and angers. You are filling yourself with the love and supportive energy to be victorious over your setbacks and to be able to create your desires and dreams. Now, say "I forgive [name of the person], I forgive myself, and I open up to the miracles that await me."

Once you get your bodies all harmonizing with one another, the next relationship you need to address is between your magnetic and dynamic energies. How your internal magnetic and dynamic energies relate directly affects how you experience your romantic relationships. Here is a favorite exercise that my clients find amazingly effective in creating that powerful internal relationship between their magnetic and dynamic energies.

A Marriage Counseling Session for Your Magnetic and Dynamic Energies

In this exercise, you'll learn how to communicate with the opposite sides of yourself—the magnetic and the dynamic—and get them to harmonize. When you do this, you will create a feeling of wholeness and balance, and open yourself up to drawing in the relationship you dream of.

Close your eyes and begin your Belly Breathing. Continue breathing, letting your body go into deeper states of relaxation. Breathe, and release.

Imagine that you are looking at the entrance to the Temple of the Dynamic and Magnetic Female. This magnificent temple is filled with a golden sun on the right and a silver moon casting a luminous glow to your left. The golden sun on the right side will activate and heal your dynamic energy, and the silver moon on the left will reawaken and nurture your Magnetic Feminine.

Feel the golden, radiant light from the sun covering the right side of your body, your dynamic side. Ask your dynamic side what he is feeling about your left, Magnetic Female side. Does he feel good about their relationship? Or does he have reservations? Let him express himself. Ask him to tell her what he needs from her. Is she willing to give it to him? If she says *yes*, let your right side open up to receive her love and support. If she says *no*, shower her with golden light. Ask her what she needs to do to let go of her negative feelings. Whatever the answer is, see if it mirrors your relationships with others.

Now, focus on your Magnetic Female side. Feel the luminous radiant energy of the silver moon pouring its shimmering light throughout the left side of your body. Ask her what she is feeling about her dynamic side. Let her respond out loud, and then listen and breathe. Does she feel good about the relationship, or does she have reservations? Keep letting her express what she is feeling.

Breathe. . . . Ask her to tell him what she needs from him. Breathe. . . . Listen. . . . Is he willing to give it to her? If he says *yes*, feel your left side receiving his love and support. If he says *no*, ask him what his fears are. Ask him out loud what he needs to do to let go of them. Whatever answer emerges, shower it with silver light and see if in any way it mirrors your relationship with others. Breathe, and continue to feel the silver light.

Focus your mind on identifying with the seamless, interactive flow of the two sides of magnetic and dynamic forces. Imagine this flow happening between your Dynamic and Magnetic Female as the silver and gold light flow into each other. Ask yourself, "Right now, which side is most dominant in my life?" Know that your dynamic and receptive energies already want to support their internal partnership from within.

Feel your Dynamic enveloping your Magnetic Female in his arms, cherishing and protecting her. Feel the nurturing and loving support she gives back to him.

Open your eyes and come back into the room. Your Dynamic and Magnetic Female are now integrated.

Just One

I find that there are many times when, after a long day of working late or spending time with my children, I need to be alone. Luckily, Edna is there to watch the twins, and I can go out by myself to eat dinner. When I show up, the host or hostess inevitably will look at me with a sympathetic smile and say "Just one?" expressing compassion for my "dismal" situation. I flash a smile, reassuring them that I'm okay. In fact, I am thrilled.

There will be many times in our lives when we won't have a romantic partner, even when we are emotionally open to having a relationship. Too often, I see women panic in this situation. They start feeling that there must be something wrong with them, and they lower their standards so that they can find a man, quick! But part of the natural rhythm of life is that sometimes you will be on your own. Seize these opportunities and embrace your independence! Connect with your dynamic force of self-reliance because it will build your confidence. Go to the movies by yourself and get comfortable sleeping alone. Work on your other dreams as you work on yourself.

If you are feeling lonely and losing faith that you will ever find the perfect partner for you, reinforce the healing energy of trust, faith, and belief by using the Power Mantras "Everything comes to me in perfect timing," "I'm drawing in the man whom I love and who loves me," or "The man who loves me is finding his way to me. He's coming as fast as he can." As you say them, release these Power Mantras into the universe in a bubble of cobalt blue light, allowing the unseen forces that are at work to bring to you what you desire.

Creating the Dream and Releasing It

With your blocks clear and your energy engaged, you're now ready to create your dream. Start with a desire and then move on to the dream. Imagine yourself in the relationship you really want. What does it look like? If it involves a particular man, that's fine. Just don't let your energies get stuck. You can make this man your preference, but not your obsession! Remember, the man you desire today might not bring you the joy and fulfillment you long for in a relationship. When Judith came to me she was in tremendous turmoil over a relationship that just ended with a man she adored. She felt that in a matter of moments everything she ever wanted in her life was taken away from her. He was very successful and was encouraging her to use her talents and work alongside him. She was feeling validated by someone who not only was very successful but whom she respected. When the relationship was over she was not only personally devastated but also felt that she could never reach a level of success her talents merited without him. I worked with her using the gold light and focused reflections to reclaim her power. Within five years she was able to climb to the top of her profession and gained greater success than she would have been able to achieve with him. If their relationship had continued, she would have always been in his shadow and would never have been acknowledged for the talent and brilliance that she owned. If you keep your intention on the qualities of the partner you want and not on who it needs to be, the universe will bring you someone who is not only special but is the exact and perfect partner to fulfill your dreams. Or you may choose to enter a relationship that will, at the very least, get you closer to what you want until the right one comes in. This kind of relationship can help you by opening you to a deeper level within yourself, allowing you to receive love and companionship and enjoy the positive shared energy of a relationship.

Energy Bath: The Love Magnet

This is a fabulous bath that you will love. It works to open up your magnetic qualities of softness, receiving, accepting, and seducing. The Love Magnet Bath will put you in the energy flow of relaxation and open receptivity so that you can draw that special partner to you with total self-confidence in your feminine power of attraction. It will also help you form a vibrational resonance with the partner you want to attract. The aromas used in these baths have a vibrational resonance, as does the water itself. Water supports the magnetic field. The qualities of bath taking—relaxing, enjoying, feeling warmth, and receiving—are all magnetic qualities. By luxuriating in this Love Magnet Bath, you will be actively receptive, expecting him to come to you, and actively patient, knowing that he will.

Place a few vanilla- or rose-scented candles around your bathroom and tub, filling the room with the soft glow of candlelight. As the water is running, sprinkle ten drops of rose or jasmine oil and gently swish the water to evenly distribute them. If you can get some rose petals (ask your florist for some), toss a handful of them into your tub. Step in and sink into the seductive and alluring waters of the Love Magnet Bath.

Close your eyes, take a deep breath in, and exhale. Continue until you feel comfortable and relaxed. Imagine that six inches above your head there is a sun of hot pink light—the color of unconditional love and expectancy of good things. Feel the rays of its radiant energy entering every cell of your body as you inhale. Allow your imagination to create the story of what it would be like to be with the partner you love. What are the qualities that you love about him? Is he generous, kind, and loving? Does he have a good sense of humor? Is he sexy? Make your list without any reservations or limitations on what you want. What happens between you and him? When do you see each other, and what do you do together? And how do you feel? Pull these images together, and once you really like what you have imagined, connect with your Field of Love, release any feelings of insecurity, fear, or doubt about having this partner come into your life, and say these Power Mantras:

+ I am a magnet of love, attracting my dreams and desires to me now.
+ I am attracting into my life a man who is loyal.
+ A man who is ready for a committed relationship is finding me.
+ I am a loving, kind, generous person, and I will receive the love I want.

Then, release your intention to the universe by sending it off through the energy of clapping your hands and saying, "And so it is." You have harnessed your dynamic forces of knowing what you want and your magnetic forces of attraction to bring you a successful outcome. My clients tell me that after doing this bath, men are smiling at them, opening doors, tripping over themselves to start a conversation, or asking for their numbers.

Dating and the Internet

If you dream of finding your soul mate, you must open up to your magnetic energy so that you can reel in plenty of potential candidates, because often it's a numbers game. Now, you might be saying, "Aleta, I hate dating! I just want to meet 'the one.'" I certainly understand that. Spending an evening with someone who is not on your frequency can be more excruciating and depressing than not having a date for New Year's Eve. You wind up glancing at your watch when you think your date isn't looking and politely smiling as you count the minutes until you can get home and crawl into your own bed.

Dating might feel like a waste of time, but it does let you see what options are out there. You'll quickly see what works for you and what doesn't. You might think you want one thing, and find out that you really need something else. That said, you don't want to get stuck going on dates that are disastrous from the first moment. Maybe you have had the experience of being set up on a blind date by a close friend who is intent on helping you find that special man. At times in my life when well-intentioned friends have set me up with potential dates that they were totally convinced would rock my world, they have been appallingly off base. And I can't tell you how many times I've heard my single clients moaning about the same scenario. So I've developed two steadfast rules for dating men you've never met before:

Get a recent photograph of the potential partner before agreeing to meet him. I'm not saying this because I think you should limit yourself to men who look like Brad Pitt or Denzel Washington. The point is to sense whether you might have any chemistry with this man, and a photograph can tell you a lot about a man's energy. Does he look anxious, withdrawn, uncomfortable, or too aggressive? Does something about him turn you off? No matter what your friends say, risk being accused of being superficial and get a recent picture.

If you are attracted, get together, but keep it short. If this is your first meeting, you don't have to sit down to an entire dinner and a movie with a stranger. Instead, you can meet him for coffee or a drink. If you immediately sense that there's no chance of a connection, you haven't invested an entire evening. I tell many of my clients who use the Internet to meet men that it's really important to get together in person for a short meeting as quickly as possible. If you get caught up in a long e-mail relationship, you might convince yourself that this man is just the one for you, and then when you finally do meet, you might have a very different reaction. Men online don't just fudge the details of what they look like and what they do for a living; they can actually create completely false personas. Sometimes you can tell this when you talk to a man on the phone—he might sound less confident than in his e-mails, for instance—but a face-to-face meeting is better for revealing who he really is. You can experience his energy, see how he communicates in person, and feel whether or not you have any connection to him.

By keeping yourself in a high vibration and following my two rules (get a picture and keep it short), you'll end up with a pretty good filter. However, a few "spammers" might get through. But know that you'll soon recognize it's a mismatch and move on quickly.

Attracting the Right Love Partner

Once you are open to your magnetic and dynamic energies and begin balancing them, you will start attracting and finding potential partners. Remember, to keep your energies flowing you must release your preconceived notions about how your dream relationship will unfold. Many of my clients have told me hilarious stories about just how unattractive they found the man of their dreams when they first met him, saying, "He totally wasn't my type—or so I thought!" I've also heard some crazy stories about how couples met. One woman's husband was the policeman who answered her call for help when she locked herself out of her car. Another happy couple I know met at a bar one night when they were both stood up on blind dates and began commiserating with each other.

Is it hard to believe that you will attract your Mr. Right? Trust me: Your personal charisma will get stronger and stronger as you keep working with the Life-Shift Tools. My clients have told me that when they really feel completely connected to their alpha and magnetic energies, people suddenly start smiling at them on the street. Strangers offer them seats on the subway. The fellows who work behind deli counters start flirting with them. One of my clients, Angie, told me she used to feel miserable when she went to dance clubs because men didn't ask her to dance and she spent the evening feeling rejected. Determined to change her energy, she revved herself up with pink light and the Power Mantra "I'm available for the right man," took a deep breath, and walked right onto the dance floor as soon as she entered a club and began undulating with the crowd. "I realized that none of these people care if I'm dancing by myself! They're having a good time, they're not looking to judge me," she told me. "And I found that when I do start dancing, inevitably some man comes up and starts dancing with me because my magnetic energy has drawn him in. Now I always dance at the clubs, and I always end up with some man's number! I know it's just a matter of time before I find the guy for me."

Know When to Be Dynamic, When to Be Magnetic, and When to Be Both

When Theresa walked into my studio, her wavy red hair flowing and piercing green eyes catching mine, she made a stunning impression. She was more than beautiful. Dressed exquisitely, Theresa had a calm, confident demeanor that would make you think she didn't have a care in the world. However, I could tell that she was very much on edge, and that it had to do with her present relationship. I asked her what was going on in her love life, and her fabulous smile faded as her eyes welled up with tears.

Then she told me, "I met a fantastic guy. We've been dating for three months and I'm crazy about him. When we're together, he seems to be crazy about me too but he doesn't make plans. The holidays are coming, and I'm not sure I'm going to be with him for New Year's Eve."

She went on to say, "I really think he's 'the one.' He'd make a perfect father. He's loving, kind, generous, and very successful. We love to do the same things, we get along great, the sex is terrific. He tells me he's not dating anyone else. So why can't he commit to this night that he knows is important to me? I want to tell him 'either you're in or you're out,' but I know that's the wrong thing to do."

I could see right away that Theresa was a woman who ran totally on dynamic energy. She confirmed my assessment when she told me she was a senior executive of a large recording company and responsible for the success of many famous artists. Her company was called Get It Done Productions. There was no question in my mind that this man was really taken with Theresa and was very interested in exploring the possibilities of the relationship. But he might be cautious and want to take his time and be sure before he totally jumped in. That was not Theresa's style.

I assured Theresa that she was absolutely right, that if she started pushing and demanding at this early stage, she was going to put him off. He needed to come to her.

"I hate that attitude!" Theresa said. "It's 1950s thinking. I should be able to just pick up the phone and ask him, 'What are we doing for New Year's Eve?' "

I told her, "That's true, you should be able to do that, but in this man's case, that's not going to work. He's challenging you to go with the flow, to let him take the lead, and to become receptive to his dynamic energy. You see, when a man is in his dynamic energy, he doesn't need you coming in with your dynamic force, pushing your way into his life. He needs to feel the absence of your energy. He needs to feel his longing for you, and he can't do that when you're a constant presence, especially if you are phoning and e-mailing him during the day. This isn't about playing a flirtation game, it's about the natural flow of energy between two people. If he's in his dynamic, and you want to be with him, you need to be in your magnetic energy, drawing him in."

I worked with Theresa, using the Life-Shift Tools of Organic

Breathing and Color Immersion. We focused on using Belly Breathing to slow her down, and the color of magnetic silver to draw to her what she desires. She was able to let go, give him space, and at the same time feel less anxious about their relationship. To her surprise, the man of her dreams called up, asking her what she was planning to do on New Year's Eve.

"You were right," Theresa told me. "He started telling me how much he'd missed me and came to realize how much he wanted me in his life. He just needed that time . . . and I needed to let go and trust and use my energy to open up and receive."

Did you ever notice that old boyfriends always seem to call once you've gotten into a new relationship? It's the same phenomenon. They sense your energy is no longer in their life, and they feel the absence that propels them to get into their dynamic energy and capture you back. Your magnetic attraction can be working even when you're not aware of it—as long as you keep it flowing, you'll draw men into your life.

Soul Mates

Many of you dream of having a soul mate, and you may well attract the soul mate you desire. Soul mates are people in your life who share a common bond and purpose and with whom you feel deeply connected. Your soul mate is someone who helps you learn your life lessons, and who teaches you about yourself. Soul mate relationships can be lovers, or they can also come in the form of siblings, good friends, or children.

As unromantic as this sounds, soul mate relationships don't always last a lifetime. It depends on what the purpose of your connection is. Once the two of you have fulfilled that purpose, your relationship may end, whether it has been going on for weeks, months, or a few years. The length of time you spend with that person has nothing to do with the importance of the relationship. The good news is that you can have more than one soul mate.

My Prince Has Come—but He's Not Always Such a Prince

Whether they are facing big problems or little disagreements, many of the couples I counsel don't know how to find common ground or work out their differences in a loving way. So many people did not have role models for good relationships, and they either mirror the bad behavior they were familiar with or, worse, create unrealistic expectations about romantic partnerships. Some of my clients expect that happy couples should never argue or get angry with each other. Trust me, there's no such thing as a long-term, loving relationship without any arguments or anger. In order to truly love someone, you need to be able to get angry at him or her once in a while and be comfortable enough to express it.

I urge my clients to give up their illusions about fairy-tale love and instead focus on learning the four insights into happy couplehood:

1. **Balance your magnetic and dynamic energies as a couple.** Any strong partnership is based on a balance of energies. You have an internal balance of magnetic and dynamic energies, and so does your partner. This allows you to give and take with each other. A truly complementary relationship is when both partners are integrated, each balancing the other's dynamic and magnetic energies. If both of you are too much in your dynamic energy, you will butt heads, always trying to get your way instead of working as a team. If both of you are too much in your magnetic energy, you'll both remain in dreamland, waiting for something to happen until finally someone has to go out and buy the gro-

ceries. If you and your partner are both operating within the same energy, you may feel very compatible but have no sexual or romantic chemistry—you're just too much alike.

Very often, I see strong, vivacious, adventurous, self-confident, and successful women enter a relationship and lose their connection to their dynamic energy. Because they believe they have to cater to the man's dynamic energy, they go too far into their magnetic. They try to draw in what they desire from their partner, but without any dynamic energy to set things in motion, nothing happens. They won't speak up and ask for what they want, and figure they'll just seduce their partner into giving them exactly what they desire, but they become disappointed because he's been left in the dark about their needs, or these women supress their own desires in order to accommodate their partners' demands. In attempting to merge in the "we," too many women give up their power and become disillusioned, unhappy, and unfulfilled.

I call this syndrome Magnetic Burnout. This situation occurs when your Magnetic Feminine starts to revolve around the dynamic alpha energy of your partner. In this situation, you draw on your magnetic energy as a constant source of love, support, and encouragement to your partner's alpha, and abandon your own dynamic forces, usually at great expense to your sense of self-worth, happiness, and well-being. Instead of sharing and harmonizing, you lose yourself in the "we."

Symptoms of Magnetic Burnout
+ Giving more than you receive
+ Overextending yourself to prove you deserve to receive
+ Feeling personally unfulfilled
+ Worrying about others' well-being at the expense of your own
+ Centering your life around your partner's visions and goals

In order to get past Magnetic Burnout, you simply need to get yourself back into balance. Reconnect with what you desire in this relationship and set your intention so that it can happen. Whatever you do, don't lose your true self.

2. **Accept and honor your partner for who he is today.** We all have our wonderful qualities and our annoying qualities! Maybe your partner is the "jump-in-there-and-deal-with-the-disaster" type, but he's not very good at foreseeing problems and avoiding them. You and your partner will drive each other batty if you can't accept each other as you are and work with it. Try to remember what initially attracted you to your partner and think of something you admire or appreciate about him. Honor him for who he is and what his needs are. You might not need to hear "I love you" every day, but if your partner does, do your best to remember to say it.

3. **Clarify your communication.** Misunderstandings are a part of any intimate relationship, but there are ways to avoid or minimize them. When you're upset, express your anger in terms of how the situation makes you feel, trusting that your partner would not want you to feel bad. Say "When you do . . . it makes me feel hurt/upset/angry, etc.," and explain why. When your partner says something that upsets you, repeat back to him what you heard and let him clarify. Say, "It sounds like what you're saying to me is that you don't want us to spend any time with my family this holiday" and listen to what he says. Maybe you heard incorrectly, and what he really said was "I don't want us to spend Christmas day with your family, just Christmas Eve."

4. **Choose to stay connected over being right.** When couples argue, each one will often go to extremes to prove that they are right. But when you are more invested in winning

the battle than in staying connected to your partner, you create a recipe for relationship disaster. You are supposed to be friends, not enemies. You can butt heads with each other and get into a competition, or you can encourage and validate each other, inspire each other, and bring out the best in each other. If you are having trouble reconnecting and working together, go back to where you first met or do something together that you used to do when you were dating, and reexperience the feelings you felt then.

The following is a wonderful exercise for helping you and your partner release your angers and negative thoughts from your emotional and mental bodies, and reconnect by bringing in your spiritual bodies.

Reconnecting Through Releasing

Decide which of the two of you will speak first. Throughout the exercise, keep eye contact at all times and do not, under any circumstances, interrupt. Take turns listening and speaking. When the exercise is over, you can ask each other questions and explore the emotions and thoughts that came up.

Sit across from each other, looking into each other's eyes. Together, imagine a golden light surrounding both of you. Take a deep breath and begin to breathe. Keeping eye contact, work together to synchronize your breathing. Continue for five solid minutes, breathing together and looking deep into each other's eyes. Whatever happens, don't say anything. Whatever feelings come up are okay. Laugh, make funny faces, just don't break eye contact.

The first partner should then express his or her feelings

about the relationship and the other person, saying "I feel angry that . . ." "I feel sad that . . ." "I feel hurt that . . ." etc. for no more than five minutes. The second partner should just listen, not asking questions, not interrupting.

When the first partner is done, the second partner should express his or her feelings about the relationship and the other person, saying "I feel angry that . . ." "I feel sad that . . ." "I feel hurt that . . ." etc.

When the second partner is finished, the first person should say, "I'm willing to work on our differences and misunderstandings. My love for you is greater than my anger. My love for you is greater than my sadness and hurt." Then the second person should say the same.

Now, the first person should express what he or she loves about the relationship and the other person, saying, "I love it when you . . ." "I get so attracted to you all over again when . . ." "I admire you so much when . . ." etc. When the first person is finished, the second person should express what he or she loves about the relationship and the other person, saying "I love it when you . . ." "I get so attracted to you all over again when . . ." "I admire you so much when . . ." etc.

When you're done, hug each other and hold on for a long time. Breathe, feeling the golden light surrounding both of you.

If your partner isn't willing to do this, you can do it on your own. Just visualize the light, breathe deeply and slowly, and speak the words you need to speak about what isn't working for you, about your willingness to make it work, and about what *is* working for you, using the language provided in the exercise.

When Relationships Are Hard to Let Go Of

Sometimes, relationships don't work out. Even if you thought you were with the man of your dreams, something might happen along the way to make you see things differently. Remember, people change, and it might be you who has made a life shift and realized that this is not the man for you. On the other hand, if he's the one to leave, it's often harder for you to accept that the relationship is over.

If you are still in love with someone you broke up with, I want to share with you a lesson I learned from my spiritual daughter, Lauren. When I first met Lauren, I was thirty and she was eight years old, with an inner beauty that radiated from the deepest part of her. Lauren and I instantly bonded over the summer, when I was staying at her house while I was performing at a summer stock theater in Plymouth, Massachusetts. She called me "Mommy Two." We used to take long walks and sing and laugh the whole way.

But on this particular day she could see I was troubled. She stopped skipping and said in a very concerned voice, "Mom, why do you look so sad?" I tried to make light of it, but Lauren wouldn't have it. "You can tell me. I understand a lot of things."

I gave her a hug and said I knew she did. I sighed and said, "I found out today that a boyfriend of mine was not being truthful to me and—"

She broke in. "He slept with someone else."

I was taken aback by her forthrightness and answered, "Yes, that's about it."

"Well," she said, "time to let him go. I don't want you to look so sad."

Tears welled up in my eyes as I told her it was not that easy, because even though I was very angry and hurt, I still loved him. And then Lauren said something that has always stayed with me. She said, "Just place him in the back part of your heart and leave the front open for someone else."

When you're not ready to release someone from your heart, remember the words of this wise little girl.

My clients find that the following Focused Reflection is an exceptionally powerful one that brings up strong, painful emotions, but can be very healing.

Time to Let Go

Inhale deeply, and exhale. Inhale, and exhale. Picture yourself on a dock on the ocean or a very large lake that you cannot see across. Tied to this dock is a raft, and on it is the person you need to release. Untie the rope and watch as the raft drifts outward toward the horizon. Say good-bye to your person. If you feel like it, you can wave and tell him or her all the things that you'll miss about them as they float off, becoming smaller and smaller until they are a speck on the horizon. Now watch as even that speck disappears.

Before you, a new speck appears, and comes closer and closer. You see it is a boat. It is bringing to you what you need. Perhaps it is a boat of healing light. Perhaps you can see who is on board, waving to you and smiling as the boat pulls up to the dock. Catch the rope as it is thrown to you, and tie the boat to the dock. Receive all that this boat has brought to you.

Overcoming Fear of Abandonment or Low Self-Worth

I've had many clients who are divorced who can't seem to get past the pain of their loss and the fear that it could happen again. They were so certain that their marriages would last forever. How can they be safe in any relationship if a marriage that was so solid could crumble and turn to dust? Even some of the women I work with who have had shorter-term relationships have experienced such a shock at the loss of what seemed like a sure thing that they can't bring themselves to believe they won't be left again.

Whenever someone hurts you, it's crucial to remember not to take it personally. So often we overlook all the many possibilities of why we were left—a midlife crisis, self-doubt, a need to find our destiny that takes us on a different path, wanting to have children when our partner doesn't, not wanting to have children when our partner does, and so on—and go right for the belief that we were abandoned because we just weren't good enough. When you've done the work of releasing your fears and letting your spiritual body rush in with its love and support, you'll *know* you can survive a breakup. You will feel stronger and more confident, and you'll know that even if you are abandoned again someday, you will never abandon yourself. You'll pick yourself up, reconnect with your four bodies, rally the troops of your Dream Team, and move on.

My client Sherry met David through an Internet dating site. Their connection was powerful from the first moment they met. They shared common values and goals, everyone told them they looked fabulous as a couple, and they even joked about how strange it was that everything in their relationship clicked. Mesmerized by each other, they found themselves in a whirlwind romance.

After three months, they began talking about their dreams and desires, and Sherry told David that after finishing up her degree she would probably move out of state, depending on where her career took her. David expressed great admiration for her talent, intelligence, and ambition. A week later David called to break a date and said something about being "really busy at work these days." When he didn't call her back for a week, Sherry called him, upset. He told her, "I think you're more into me than I am into you." Sherry listened in shock, unable to take it in. What had happened?

I told Sherry, "I think this man really felt for you all the things he said he felt. But he got scared. When he was faced with the reality that you'll move across the country, and that he'd have to decide whether to go with you or carry on a long-distance romance or break up, he bolted. He figured he'd protect himself from being hurt in the future by leaving you before you could leave him."

Sherry admitted this made sense, and she tried to get David to talk to her about his insecurities, but he ignored her calls and e-mails. It became apparent that she would have to move on. But emotionally she couldn't stop feeling that she must have done something wrong and began to replay and retrace the last time they were together. She asked me with such pain in her heart, "How could he take something so wonderful and just throw it away?" After working with her for several months, the worst of the trauma was behind her and she said to me, "I know I've got to get back out there and date again. But how can I let myself be vulnerable? How can I trust again?"

I had Sherry continue to release her fears into cobalt blue light and reinforce the positive, healing energy of the light by saying the Power Mantra "There's someone better coming for me." It may sound funny, but Sherry also began to release her fear of abandonment and reinforce her belief that she was strong enough to get past this by listening to Gloria Gaynor's recording of "I Will Survive" and singing along. "My voice breaks and I burst into sobs, but inside I keep singing along until I feel like I really *can* survive," she said.

Releasing Feelings of Abandonment

Inhale, and exhale. Place your hands on your heart, and continue breathing. Ask yourself, What am I feeling? Where am I holding this feeling? What thoughts am I holding on to in my mental body? When you are in touch with the emotions and thoughts that are feeding your fear of abandonment, release those toxins into the light. Draw in the support of your nurturing, spiritual body. Feel it rush in with its unconditional love as you say the Power Mantra "I am love. I am loved. I am loving."

What You Had, What You Deserve

When someone has just left you and you're feeling abandoned, write down a list of the things that your ex-partner did or didn't do in the relationship that made you unhappy. List what didn't work about his or her relationship with you. Really be honest. Check your list any time you find yourself resisting the memory of the bad times. Did this person lie to you? Did he belittle you or what you hold dear? Did he break his promises?

Now, on a new piece of paper, start making a list of what you want in your dream relationship: honesty, respect for your choices and beliefs, and so on. Keep writing until you feel you've listed all the qualities you are seeking in a partner.

Compare your lists and see how much of a difference there is between the two lists! Focus on the positive list. Now that you know what you want, bring it into your life. Create a new dream for a better relationship and release your vision into your Field of Love.

You Gotta Have Friends

Right now there is no man in my life, and although I look forward to bringing in a great new love at some point, for now I am happy to be sharing the love that I have with my two children. My Dream Team is taking care of all three of us, and we are all physically, mentally, emotionally, and spiritually thriving. I have my two beautiful twins, I have my family, and I have my friends. I am satisfied and content.

When the good men are nowhere to be found, remember that you will always have your friends. We have been so programmed to be on the lookout for men that we often forget about the roles our female friends can play. One of these women might actually be a soul mate, or at least a permanent member of your Dream Team. As long as you all don't enter the Chat Room of Discontent, your female friends can be just as supportive and nurturing as any man (and often more so!).

Whenever you feel especially thankful for your friends, say the following Power Prayer: "Thank you for the women in my life, and for the support network I have built."

Remember that love and support come in many forms and from many sources. Be sure to stay open and receive all the love that comes to you. Love is life's greatest gift.

8

THE HEART OF SEX

Spring 1952, Brooklyn

I was five years old when my father announced that he was taking me to see the top of the world, the Empire State Building. An adventure with my dad was always a magical experience, and I couldn't stop giggling. Once we got to "the city," we found ourselves on a crowded, bustling street. I strained my neck upward until I felt as if it would break, but I still couldn't see the top of the Empire State Building. It looked like an incredible silver bullet soaring up into perfect clouds and blue sky.

As soon as we entered the majestic building and the silver elevator doors closed, I fell silent. My father and I were surrounded by a group of women, perfumed creatures whose painted faces and large melon breasts made me wonder aloud, "What do you think and feel when you get to be that big?"

My dad laughed off my comment and squeezed my sweaty palm. I could feel my eyes grow wider as I realized this is what I would grow up to be. I pulled excitedly at my father's arm and blurted out, "Dad, what's more important to a woman, her vagina or her heart?"

The Heart of Sex

There was a quiet gasp and the women seemed to freeze, their eyes trained on my father, waiting for his response. After what seemed like an eternity, he looked directly into my eyes and said, "Well, Aleta, they are both very important; one creates life and one sustains it."

Sometimes it takes a lifetime to really understand the complexity of such an innocent question—and to see the wisdom in my dad's response. For many women, reconciling their own sexuality is one of the biggest challenges they face—and one of the most difficult to talk about.

Believe me, I understand the double messages of sexuality. I was raised Catholic. Need I say more? While I've always had a very open and healthy attitude about sex, at one point in my life, I actually wanted to become a nun!

Of course, things changed. By the time second grade rolled around, I was already in love with the boy who yanked my ponytail, which quickly ended my early engagement to the Lord. At twelve I was stuffing my bra along with my other girlfriends on the way to mass and wondering which cute boys were going to show up. At the same time, we were beginning to hear all sorts of mixed messages about sex. We were supposed to wait until marriage to make love, and tongue-kissing was considered a mortal sin for which you would roast in hellfire eternally.

The start of my active sexual life coincided with the "free love" generation of the late 1960s, and I was all too happy to just go with the flow. When I got the lead in Hair at age twenty-one, my immediate family flew to Amsterdam to see me perform. My mother was shocked when she saw that the first act culminated in a nude scene. When it was over, she quietly asked me, "Aleta, can't you get a better job?" But as people started to congratulate her on my great performance, she accepted it as part of "show business" and being a hippie, and returned to being my greatest supporter. I must admit that there was a moment as I lay under the parachute right before the nude scene when I thought, "Maybe I don't have to do this today in front of my family." But after only a moment's hesitation I realized I had to be true to my beliefs and the message of the *play, and I emerged with the rest of the cast, singing "Beads, Flowers, Freedom, Happiness" and closed the first act, baring all.*

Reclaiming Your Sexuality

Don't be embarrassed if your big dream is to fully experience your sexual desires. I applaud you for targeting something so integral to your life. In fact, I find that in my practice, reclaiming sexual energy is a common theme of what many women long for. All too often, women say that they have a low sex drive, much more so than men. It's amazing to me that in a study done by the *Journal of the American Medical Association,* it was estimated that twenty-four million American women aren't interested in sex.

Honestly, I don't think this number is correct. I believe that for most of these women, the problem isn't that they aren't interested in sex; it's that they have never been given the opportunity to fully explore a satisfying sex life. This lack of experience can have several outside causes, including lack of sexual partners, partners who are poor performers, or true physical limitations.

However, most of the blocks to great sex occur within ourselves. Many of my clients who have been married or in relationships for a long time come to see me because they are bored with their sexual life (sounds like a mental body block, right?). Here's another: They say they are burned out from the rest of the dynamic energy demands placed on them, including raising a family and/or having to work. When I start to talk to them about what they can practically and energetically do to get their sex life back on track, they look at me, totally exhausted, and say, "Aleta, the last thing that I have any energy or desire for is sex! I couldn't care less." Believe me, I hear what they are saying. After having had my twins, even I've joked with my more experienced mommy friends and asked, "Am I ever going to want to have sex again?"

Your Inner Seductress

Unblocking the toxins from the physical, emotional, or mental body is the first step to reclaiming or beginning a great sex life. But more important, sexual disinterest can usually be directly related to lost or unsupported Magnetic Feminine energy. Without it, you will not have the ability to attract great sex to you, to be patient when it comes to you, or to be able to intuitively know what it is that turns you on. These are the three most important aspects of a great sex life, and they are yours for the taking once you tune in and turn on your Magnetic Feminine energy. When this happens, you will have tapped into your inner seductress.

Many of my clients say that once they have used their Life-Shift Tools and gotten back in touch with their Magnetic Feminine and aligned it properly with their dynamic energy, their sexual energy and desire return—or are ignited—in full force. These women say that they feel regenerated and have more vitality. They look and feel younger and have an inner and outer youthful glow. When our sexual energy flows freely, whether we use it for sexual connection or we redirect it toward some creative project, it can invigorate us. Have you ever put on a CD to energize yourself while you clean or organize your home? Or listened to soul music and felt the sudden urge to get up and sway your hips and snap your fingers? This is because you are responding to the sexual energy in the music.

Those of my romantically involved clients who have worked with me to recharge their sexual energy report that they feel a renewed connection with their partners. They also say that as a couple, they are more loving and attentive toward each other. This is because the sexual connection helps them break through their mental and emotional walls and, as a result, connect with a deeper intimacy. The profound sense of oneness we can achieve through sexual union not only connects us to ourselves and our partners, but to the cosmic flow of our Field of Love.

You might be saying, "Oh come on, Aleta, are you saying that sex is spiritual?" You got it! Sexual energy is one of the most ancient expressions of the spiritual self. Eastern cultures have known this for thousands of years, and their connection to sexual energy can be seen in their artwork and the sculptures of their deities. In today's world, sexual energy can be just as important, as long as you make it a priority.

When you are in true union with someone, it is one of the closest feelings to the spiritual flow of creation that you will ever get.

Connecting Your Sexual Energy to Your Physical Body

It's true that someone or something can "turn you on" and ignite your passion, but sexuality is also an internal, sensual vitality that you can draw on any time. As with everything that you have been learning in this book, feeling the passion of your sexual energy is an *inside job.* By awakening your internal fire, you can improve your sex life, energize one that may be limping along, and reconnect to your desire for sexual fulfillment and build up your sexual self-esteem.

Over the years, I have learned a lot about my own sexuality as well as how to help others get in touch with theirs. Several years ago I was given a wonderful opportunity to write a sex advice column and magazine feature articles for the men's magazine *American Health and Fitness.* The demographics of the readers were men between the ages of twenty-five and thirty-five. I was excited about the potential . . . what a great opportunity to help young women have fabulous sex by enlightening men on the ways to be better lovers.

Perhaps you may be feeling that the fire within has dwindled away to a small ember. Here's the first secret I shared with the boys at

The Heart of Sex

American Health and Fitness so that we can rekindle your fire—experiencing extraordinary sex begins with the physical body. You appreciate and enjoy the beauty of life by using the five senses of smell, touch, taste, seeing, and hearing. The taste of good food, the texture of a soft, silky robe, and the soothing aroma of jasmine not only feed your senses, they reconnect you with your sexual force. By stimulating your five senses, you will exercise your physical qualities, which will allow you to open the way through the emotional and mental bodies and let the spiritual energy flow through you.

On the island of Mallorca, off the coast of Spain, I once met a very mysterious man who introduced me to the sensual powers of food. After we had danced all night, he suggested we cool off at the beach . . . the sun was just coming up as we walked onto the cool, damp sand. A native of the island was setting up his fruit stand, and my friend bought a large bunch of plump, juicy grapes. We strolled to the edge of the water and sat down on the rocks. The magic happened as he began feeding me those grapes . . . slowly, one by one. Years later, I still remember that man!

One of the main qualities of your Magnetic Female is your ability to draw to you what you desire. The exercise on the following page can help you get in touch with your inner seductress through enjoying the sensuality of your physical body.

Sensual Delights

+ Lie naked on a bed, and visualize the pink light of unconditional love wrapping itself around you. Connect with your Energizing Breathing by inhaling and exhaling in a slow rhythm, with the exhalations lasting a bit longer than the inhalations. Brush a feather, feather boa, silk, or other soft and sensuous material against your skin, rubbing it in a circular motion over your belly, your breasts, your thighs, your toes, and the base of your neck. Feel the energy of pink light permeating every cell of your body, releasing any blocks you have toward enjoying the experience and allowing yourself to receive it. Experiment with using a light touch or a deeper touch to see which is more pleasurable to you.

+ Certain foods are very sensuous. Prepare a tray for yourself featuring sensual foods you know you enjoy, including oysters on the half shell, honey, and wet fruits like mango, papaya, and watermelon. Envision yourself and the food surrounded by a bubble of royal purple light, the color of expansion. Royal purple will enhance and intensify the flavors and textures of the foods. If you are experiencing these foods with your romantic partner, loosely cover your eyes with a tie or a silk eye mask while your partner places the food on your lips and tongue, leaving you guessing what tasty delight you are experiencing. Use your magnetic energy to draw in and enjoy the sensual pleasure of the food.

+ Play soulful, energetic music, such as R&B or salsa, that inspires you to dance and let the sound move through your body. Envision a glowing, ruby red sun in front of you, radiating its energy into your body, from your feet all the way to the top of your head. Connect to the rhythm of the music and dance. Visualize your feet drawing energy from the earth as you move.

(cont.)

+ If you are inhibited or feel stiff, stand up and bend your knees slightly and move your hips in a figure eight, or imagine yourself swirling a hula hoop or riding a horse, whatever will help you get a fluid motion going. Moving the pelvis center of your sexual energy will start to release your inner sexual energy.

+ Try making love to different types of music to see which ones open you to feeling a sense of sexual self-expression. If you usually listen to soul music, try rock and roll. If you usually listen to New Age music, put on a jazz CD. See which types inspire your inner seductress to tap into her sexuality.

+ Instead of making love on the bed, you can get yourself sensually enhanced by having sex on a furry rug or throw, in the shower, or on a towel on the grass outside (if you have privacy!). Make love under different kinds of light—candlelight, firelight, the waning light of sunset, or the soft light of sunrise. Get out of your norm, and for everyone's sake, get out of the dark! One of my clients had a particularly hot experience making love while a flashing neon sign lit up the room.

+ Wear clothing that makes you feel sexy, whether it's a flowing, silky nightgown; a lacy, plunging bra; a teddy and garters; or a Brazilian thong. And for those of you who are more adventurous, take the plunge and get a Brazilian bikini wax (by a professional—do not attempt to do this yourself!).

+ The next time you make love to your partner, focus on the sensations of the experience. Notice how you enjoy being touched. Experience your partner's skin—what is its texture, its temperature, its color? What does your partner's hair smell like? What sounds does your partner make as you kiss? Taste his lips. Talk to your partner—tell him what sensations you are enjoying. Feel yourself present, in your body, savoring this experience.

Physical problems such as hypothyroidism, depression, or hormonal imbalances can also short-circuit your libido. If your sexual drive has been nonexistent for a long time, it's a good idea to check out these possibilities with a physician. If that is not the case, think about the likelihood that you are suffering from dynamic burnout. After putting the kids to sleep, you often have just about enough energy to fall into bed, completely fatigued. Consequently, you have little or no interest in sex. As you push sex to the back burner, you may lose the desire for it altogether, which turns the situation into a vicious cycle. Once your physical body has been restarted by awakening your senses, try the following exercise as a great second step toward a more sexual you. These small actions can go a long way toward reconnecting you to your sexuality and freeing your inner seductress to work her magic.

Rev Your Engine

+ Take the time to slow down and make spending time with your loved one a priority. Make a point of reconnecting every day, even if it's just for ten minutes in the morning.
+ Get some kind of stretching or exercise routine going, along with a nutritional program, so that you feel good about your body and connected to it, instead of living in your mental or emotional body all the time.
+ Get a babysitter—call upon your Dream Team, or take turns with other couples, giving one another time off from child care.
+ Find the time for you and your partner to give each other a twenty-minute massage with your favorite oil.
+ Shower together. Lather each other up. Afterward, spend ten minutes in bed together, just holding each other.

Ignite Passion in the Mental Body

Our mental body can be blocked when we are overly critical of ourselves or are not able to ask for what we need. One of the most common mental obstacles to great sex is having a poor body image. It is a great myth that only gorgeous, sexy, slim women have extraordinary sex lives. It boggles my mind how many beautiful women feel they are sexually inadequate because they look in the mirror and don't see Angelina Jolie staring back at them. I have clients who've told me that they can't imagine how a man would want to sleep with them with their fat thighs (which is more often than not a distorted perception of what they actually look like). When a man is in the throes of sexual passion, he's not taking out a magnifying glass to assess your physical landscape. If anything, he's hoping that he is "hot" enough to turn you on. While writing my "Sex Files" column, I was amazed at the number of questions I got from men who were feeling pressured about their ability to perform. Women are worried about cellulite and men are worried about their size or whether they have the right techniques. If each partner focuses on sharing their love, these concerns melt away as the passion heats up.

If you are feeling uncomfortable with being less than perfect, don't make love under a fluorescent light with mirrors all around you. Other than that, go for it! Great sex is a matter of connection—connecting with the passion of your heart and soul and then beaming that love toward your partner.

If you find it difficult to embrace the beauty and sensuality of your body, the first step is to accept your body and love it as it is right now. The following exercise will help you to experience your physical body as it expresses your spirit.

Let Your Body Express Your Spirit

After you have taken a bath or shower, towel yourself dry with a big, soft towel. Remain naked, and sit or lie on your bed. Take a deep breath in, and exhale. Inhale, and exhale any tensions. Feel the energy of your spiritual body coming into you, infusing you with the radiance of warm orange light.

Squeeze some body lotion into your hands. Rub the lotion into your face, saying "My face expresses my beauty. My spiritual body expresses itself in my face. I love my face." Now, rub lotion into your neck, saying "My neck expresses my beauty. My spiritual body expresses itself in my neck. I love my neck." Continue to say these Power Mantras, rubbing lotion into all the parts of your body, working your way from your head to your toes. Keep envisioning that radiant orange light of regeneration coursing through your body, surrounding you with love and acceptance.

When you are finished, hug yourself tightly and say "My spirit is expressing itself through my body. I am a magnet, and I can attract men to me. I accept my body as it is today. I love my body, and I am working to eat better and exercise more."

Notice the areas of your body that you feel uncomfortable praising. The next time you do this exercise, pay special attention to those areas, saying the Power Mantras about those parts of your body several times before moving on.

As you learn to love your body and let your spirit express itself, avoid comparing yourself to magazine photographs of "perfect" models. In person, no model is truly flawless. A lot of money and time is spent creating those artificial images, including expensive (and often uncomfortable) beauty treatments and computer retouching. And don't forget that what men perceive as sexy can be exactly the opposite of these glossy pictures. What's more, I've found that men and women often don't agree on what is appealing.

If you don't love your body, there may be a reason for it. Is your body out of shape, tired, and not functioning well? If so, start exercising and improving the way you eat. Treat your body well, and it will be much easier to connect to your sexual energy.

Not Knowing What You Want and Need

Most women have a better idea of how to pleasure a man than how to pleasure themselves. Many are unaware of their body's sexual response—what makes them start to feel hot and what sends them over the edge. It's no wonder, when the images of "great sex" that we see in the movies show the woman reaching orgasm about two seconds after the leading man starts kissing her! It's enough to make anyone start to feel inadequate when their own experiences take far longer!

When we are not connected to our Magnetic Feminine energy, we lose our intuitive knowledge about what makes us feel good during sex. We also lose the ability to draw this knowledge inward. If you're not sure how to experience sexual pleasure, or how to help a partner sexually arouse you and bring you to orgasm, use your Magnetic Feminine energy to seek help. There are plenty of informational books, magazines, and instructional videos about sexuality that can give you straight answers to your questions. Allow yourself to explore your body and discover what feels good to you. Sex therapists can offer invaluable advice. But please, don't turn to fiction, either in books or in movies, for the answers. These scenarios are not real, even if they sound or look great. Patience is also an attribute of the Magnetic Feminine. Often, you just have to wait a minute before your fire starts. Real people take time to turn on.

Not Asking for What You Want or Need

Once you know what will give you sexual pleasure, it's important to be able to ask for it. Men are not mind readers, and besides, every woman is unique and responds to touches, sounds, and movements differently. One of my clients remembers a particularly good, experienced lover telling her, "I don't know what will turn you on. You'll have to show me. But I promise I'm a very eager learner!"

Not all men have such confidence. From having answered letters in my sexual advice column, I can reassure you that all men want to be Casanovas, but many are just as anxious and nervous about their sexual skills as you may be. So what's the best way to communicate what you need? Use your Magnetic Feminine energy to make a connection with your lover. Then use your dynamic forces to:

+ Talk to your partner when you're not in the process of making love. When the two of you are bonding together, kissing lightly and hugging, tell him, "You know, I just love it when you . . ." or "Let's try something" and introduce a new activity. Or teasingly say, "Why don't we [name an activity that turns you on]? Because, you know, that just drives me wild!" If you talk to him about what you like while you're in the act, he may get intimidated or embarrassed, or become mechanical as he tries too hard to "follow the directions."

+ Tell him what turns you on rather than what turns you off. If you feel you have to tell him not to do something, say "I'm uncomfortable when you [name the action], but I love it when you [name something he can do instead]." For instance, you may like larger, slower, more circular movements, or you may want to "warm up" by just having your partner run his hands over your naked body. If you can, try to express your discomfort with the action, not with him—say "I get uncomfortable when my skin is touched lightly" rather than "When you touch my skin lightly, I get uncomfortable."

+ Let yourself moan and make whatever other sounds come up when you are enjoying sex. Often, this can communicate to a man "That's working for me!" even better than words could.
+ If you feel very tongue-tied, consider buying a sex guide or an erotic novel and leaving it on the nightstand, and bookmark the page you'd like him to read. You might say to him, "I heard about this book and it's really hot. Do you want me to read some of it to you?"

Now, one annoyance that some of my clients have experienced is that no matter how often and in how many ways they communicate their sexual needs to their partner, he doesn't listen—or he doesn't consistently follow through. Maybe he'll go along with her wishes once or twice, but then she has to ask again, constantly, until she gets deeply frustrated. If this is the case with you and your partner, ask yourself how important sex is to you. If it is important to you, make sure he knows your feelings. Suggest that you go together to see a sex therapist, and if he refuses, think deeply about how much longer you want to be with someone who doesn't care about something as important as what gives you pleasure.

Your Sexy Mental Body

You can stimulate your mental body by reading erotic books and making up fantasies that turn you on. Give yourself permission to have explicit sexual fantasies. Remember, every woman thinks about sex, so you are not the only one who has fantasies. Maybe you want to experience being the chaste maiden deflowered by her prince, or you want to imagine being a powerful sexual goddess who seduces a stranger. Draw on your magnetic creativity and pay attention to the response of your physical body. Once you've opened up to the flow of your sexual energy, take it wherever you want to take it.

Talk to others who are very comfortable with their sex lives. Ask your girlfriends what they are doing to expand on their sexual experiences and fantasies. You'd be surprised at how you can inspire one another to reach new heights of passion and creativity. Use these close friends as your sexual Dream Team, becoming a powerful resource to one another by giving yourselves permission as well as inspiration.

When the Honeymoon Ended Before the Bags Were Unpacked

Surprisingly, there are couples I have worked with who had a great sexual life before they got married, and as soon as they were on their honeymoon they found that their partner was no longer sexually interested in them. This can be very devastating. Often what has happened is that once a couple is married, each views their partner differently. While it was okay to enjoy having sex before the marriage, they might feel uncomfortable now that they will be role-playing a lifestyle more like that of their parents. Or they might have felt less vulnerable to having expressive sex when they were in a more loosely committed situation. Whatever the case, these mental and emotional roadblocks don't have to last long. Go back to the exercises in the mental body section of Chapter 4, and reexamine the Focused Reflections as a couple. If that doesn't help, you may want to seek the advice of a trained professional marriage counselor before the honeymoon really *is* over.

Getting the Mind Out of the Way

Sometimes, we just think too much. This is especially true in relation to sex. Overthinking anything is a lot like worrying, which is definitely a dynamic mental block. When you begin to panic, or overthink how or why you are having sex a particular way, especially when you are actively engaged in it, you are too much in your alpha energy and too much in your head. You need to quiet your mind and bring it into harmony with your physical, emotional, and spiritual bodies.

The following Focused Reflection is a quick tool to get you out of your head and back into your body so that you can enjoy the full sexual experience.

Learn how to do this exercise now, so that when you need it you will be ready. You can do this right before you have sex.

Using your Release Breathing, let go of any anxieties you may have with each exhalation. Quiet your mind by imagining a helium balloon filled with radiant violet light, hovering over your head. Breathe into this light, and with every exhalation, blow your worries into the balloon. Feel how much lighter your mind is, and watch the balloon float away from you until it is so small that you can barely see it. Now, take a deep breath and hold it for a count of five. Reconnect with your physical body while you are holding your breath. Exhale, and say to yourself the following Power Mantra: "I am ready to let go and experience amazing sex."

The Emotional Angle

Our emotional body can be blocked by holding on to past or current hurts and/or anger. Most of the couples I work with who are having sexual problems really have a relationship problem that's showing up in the bedroom. Their communication skills need work, or they don't honor each other's differences and work together as a couple. When communication fails, and couples don't work at being a team, it is only natural that they will have misunderstandings and hurt feelings, hostilities and resentments. They emotionally distance themselves from each other and, as a result, close down sexually. Even if they continue having sex, it's unfulfilling and lonely for both of them. When this happens, both parties need to make a commitment to themselves and to the relationship to work out the roadblocks toward intimacy they may be experiencing. If you find yourself in this space, revisit the emotional relationship exercise in Chapter 7 and clear your blocks so that you can connect back with your sexual energy.

Fear of Being Hurt Again

I have seen many clients who have gone through long periods without having sex, or who are still holding on to past infidelities and betrayals. The idea of putting themselves in a vulnerable situation sends them running in the opposite direction. They figure if they keep their passion fires dim, they won't be tempted to get into a relationship where they could get hurt again. They have closed down emotionally and sexually.

Deborah, a client of mine, had been married for twelve years and had three wonderful children whom she adored. Her husband was a vibrant man who had made a fortune in the stock market and had been able to retire at age forty. They were like a storybook couple—

always out socially, smiling and laughing together. Their love for each other was contagious, and people always wanted to be around them. However, when Deborah went out of town to visit her parents one weekend, her husband drank too much and a good friend of theirs took this as an opportunity to seduce him. When Deborah found out through their housekeeper, she was devastated and heartbroken. No matter how much she tried, she just couldn't bring herself to forgive her husband. She couldn't believe that if he really loved her he could sleep with another woman. He pleaded with her and begged her forgiveness and was truly sorry that he had deeply hurt her, but nothing he could say helped. The passion she once felt for him turned cold. She couldn't bear for him to touch her, and when he did, the orgasms that had once come so effortlessly were now nonexistent.

I encouraged her to place her hand on her heart and breathe deeply, inhaling gold light and bringing its energy into that part of her body that was holding on to her negative feelings toward him. I had her express her hurt and rage at her husband so that she could let go of those emotional toxins. Deborah then placed her hands on her pelvis, where the sexual center is located, described what she was feeling, and breathed out the cold numbness. Deborah continued to cry as she released her anger at her husband's selfish behavior.

At the end of her session, Deborah felt emotionally and physically spent, but relieved and lighter. I then asked her to try to feel the love that her husband had for her and draw that into her heart. Every day, she would constantly repeat the Power Mantra "I'm open to embrace the love that you have for me" and envision the powerful energy of emerald green light circling back and forth between her husband's heart and hers, continually connecting them.

Over the next few months, her sexual energy started to return sporadically, until one day she saw her husband playing with their children. All of a sudden the love that she felt for him became stronger than her need to push him away and punish him. Before long, they were able to heal their relationship and make their love even stronger.

Are there any sexual wounds that you are holding on to—betrayals, infidelities, or perhaps abuse or rape? It's important that you release and heal these traumas. If they are particularly troubling, strong wounds, consider approaching an energy therapist, talk therapist, or minister whom you feel you can trust, and asking him or her to help you to move through the fears, hurts, and angers you might still be holding on to.

If you find yourself having this problem, revisit the relationship chapter and do the forgiveness exercise until you feel like you have shifted your energy.

Shamed and Confused

Often, our parents tried to scare us and make us feel negative about our sexuality because they were trying to protect us. In my day, being an unwed mother was a terrible stigma, especially for young women. Girls who were said to be "doing it" were called easy, or cheap, even by their friends. Today, women feel damned if they do and damned if they don't—if they have sex, they're "slutty"; if they don't have sex, they're "prudes." The potential for losing the approval of friends and family for being sexual can make a woman disconnect from her sexuality, feeling ashamed or confused every time she feels her passion begin to rise.

If you carry feelings of shame about your sexuality, the following Focused Reflection can help you get at the root of your blocks and release the emotions and beliefs that are holding you back. However, if you are a survivor of rape, sexual abuse, or incest, or suspect you might be, I strongly suggest you do this exercise under the supervision of a therapist or minister who can help you release and heal the feelings that may come up.

Shame Release

Inhale deeply and slowly, and exhale. Inhale, and as you exhale, let go of any tensions. Place your hands over your pelvic area, the center of your sexual energy. Continue breathing deeply and let any feelings of shame come up.

Ask yourself, "When was this shame instilled in me?" In your mind's eye, return to that time. What do you see happening? Is a lover saying something to you that makes you feel ashamed? Are your teenage peers gossiping about developing bodies or about sexual experiences? Are they talking about you? Are you seeing something on television or in a movie or magazine that makes you feel excited and then ashamed of your body or your sexuality? Is a preacher or minister, gym or health teacher, scout leader, or doctor telling you something about sexuality that makes you feel ashamed? Is someone you know asking you to do something with your body that you don't want to do?

As you feel these thoughts and emotions come up, ask yourself, "What negative role does this shame play in my life today? Might there be a more joyful way to live my life than to hang on to shame?"

Take a deep breath, and visualize a fiery ball of gold light in front of you. Exhale, and release the feeling of shame into the light. Watch it disintegrate in the fire. Feel the unconditional love and acceptance of your spiritual body as it floods you with its light and energy. Say "My sexuality is a beautiful and powerful gift waiting to be shared."

The Ultimate Spiritual Connection

I believe that sexuality is not really about sex, but more about having a soul-centered sexual experience in which our passion and sensuality connect with the ecstasy of our heart. Unless you connect sex with your heart, mind, body, and spirit, you will never feel satisfied and fulfilled, no matter how many sexual techniques you know or how many great lovers you have.

The following exercise will help you feel this energy connection.

Red Light Connection

The next time you are making love with a man, as you take him in, picture ruby red light coming from your tailbone, and infusing both you and your lover, coursing through your body, and feel an exchange of energy from your pelvis to his.

One of the most important aspects of your energy connection to your partner is balancing your magnetic and dynamic energies so that you can enjoy the giving and receiving of sexual pleasure. One of my clients, Sally, was too much into her dynamic energy, and as a result, whenever she made love to a new partner, she was trying too hard to have an orgasm. She felt she "should" be able to have at least one, every time, so from the moment she and her partner began touching or kissing, she would begin thinking, "Okay, prepare yourself. This time, you're going to come."

Well, needless to say, with all that pressure, Sally wasn't able to relax and let go. Her mind went into overdrive, trying to figure out what was "wrong" with her. Her partner didn't comment on it, but she was afraid he'd think she was frigid, so after a few weeks she began faking orgasms. By the time she came to me for healing work, she'd been faking them for two years.

"He has no idea what an acting job I'm doing! I can't let him know, but I'm so frustrated and dissatisfied," she told me. "It's a mess—what do I do now?"

We had talked about her physical health, and neither of us felt that was a problem. Sally did have some emotional and mental blocks that we were working on, but I said to her, "Sally, I think your main obstacle is that you are too much into your dynamic energy. You're not surrendering to the experience of lovemaking. You're trying to direct it too much. I think what you should do is not fake it, and not let yourself try to have an orgasm. Instead, I want you to focus on the feeling of silver light coursing through your body, attracting your lover, as you mentally repeat the Power Mantra 'Relax, let go, and receive.' Every time you start to think about having an orgasm, or about whether he thinks you're getting excited, breathe and switch your mind over to repeating that Power Mantra and feel your body just giving over to having pleasure.

"You might be surprised," I said. "Just slow down and savor the sensations as you connect with him. Be in the moment as you kiss him and look him in the eye. If your body starts responding, repeat your Power Mantra: 'Relax, let go, and receive.' "

When Sally saw me again, I wasn't surprised to hear what had happened. "I did exactly what you said, Aleta. And the first couple of times, it was hard. By the third time I did it, I suddenly felt myself on a plateau, and then I had this moment of feeling weightless, and suddenly my whole body started shaking, and moans were coming out of my mouth that I couldn't believe were mine!"

Sally had discovered the power of bringing in her magnetic energy to balance her dynamic, and this had unblocked the flow of her sexual energy. After that, she didn't have to fake orgasms because her four bodies were working in concert to help her achieve them.

Tantric Energy Circle

This is an exercise based on tantric ideas of harmonizing your sexual energies with a partner. Both you and your partner will use your dynamic and magnetic energies to send energy to each other and draw in energy from each other. You'll be working with the colors of your energy centers: ruby red for the sexual center (located in the pelvis) and emerald green for the heart center; indigo, or purplish blue, for the mental center, in the forehead; and white for the spiritual center, at the top of your head.

Lie down next to your partner, facing each other. Both of you can be naked or clothed, whichever you prefer. Look deep into your partner's eyes, and maintain your eye contact during this exercise.

As you lie together, synchronize your breathing. Fall into a rhythm that feels comfortable for both of you. Inhale together. Exhale together, maintaining your loving gaze with each other.

When you are ready, each of you should place your right hand on the other's tailbone. Imagine a red ball of light at the base of your spine as you breathe. With your partner, feel that energy getting stronger and stronger. Now, send it out with your right hand, using your dynamic energy. Then, using your magnetic energy, receive the red light that your partner sends you through his hand. Feel this energy moving throughout your whole pelvic area as you continue to dynamically send the red light to your partner and magnetically pull it in from him.

Continue exchanging energy and breathing for at least ten minutes, even if it feels awkward. If either of you begins to feel aroused, don't act on your energy—just keep breathing and let it build.

Now, I want you to imagine this red, passionate energy moving up your spine and locating itself in your heart, where it transforms into emerald green. Place your right hand on your partner's heart as he places his right hand on yours. Send this emerald green light to him with your right hand, using your dynamic energy. Then, using your magnetic energy, receive the emerald green light that your partner, using his dynamic energy, sends you through his hand. Feel this energy moving and filling your heart center.

Continue exchanging energy and breathing. Now feel your heartfelt sexual energy rising from your pelvis and moving up through your heart to the center of your forehead, where it changes to a deep indigo light. Place your right hand on the back of his head and have your partner place his right hand on the back of your head. Feel your dynamic energy beaming an indigo light from your forehead into his, and with your magnetic energy, draw in the indigo light he is sending you with his dynamic energy. Continue to move this circle of energy between the two of you, both of you switching back and forth between your dynamic and magnetic energies.

Now, place your right hand on the top of his head and have your partner place his right hand on the top of your head. Feel your dynamic energy beaming a white light from the top of your head into his, and with your magnetic energy, draw in the white light he is sending you with his dynamic energy. Continue to move this circle of energy between the two of you, both of you switching back and forth between your dynamic and magnetic energies.

You might be saying, "Aleta, if I ever suggested that to my partner, he would think I had gone off the deep end." You are right, many men would say something like this, so what I've done myself, and have suggested to my clients, is to project the colors to him while you are making love. Without fail, it definitely revs up the passion in the most macho of men.

By getting back into your Magnetic Feminine energy, your once-hidden sexuality will come out and shine. Your dynamic energy will support your feminine, and you will be able to life shift and become one with your inner seductress whenever you want. What's more, your balanced sexual energy will be able to enhance your creativity in every aspect of your life. Enjoy!

9

RECEIVING ABUNDANCE: ATTRACTING MONEY AND A FABULOUS CAREER

2005, New York City

Before I ever considered having children, I was a busy single woman living in New York City. I considered myself to be financially successful: I had the freedom to do whatever I wanted, and somehow I could always afford it. I had an assistant, an office, a full practice, and was able to live a prosperous lifestyle in a city where a rent of $4,000 per month for a small two-bedroom apartment was considered a steal.

However, at fifty-three, when I started seriously pursuing having a child, I realized that I would have to create a larger financial base to draw from if I wanted to give this child the very best available in one of the most expensive cities in the world. I knew that in order to make this happen, I would first have to create a financial life shift. For me, making money was never really a motivating force, and I never felt that I needed the security of having gobs of it in the bank. I had never thought of looking at numbers from a bottom-line perspective. I always followed my heart, and financially things worked out.

I knew that I would need to be motivated in order to manifest a larger financial base, and it would have to come from something my heart truly desired. I thought about my dream of having a child and realized that this dream would serve as the best incentive for creating financial security for my new family, with or without a man's help.

I started to pursue this desire with my self-confidence intact and my dynamic and magnetic energies perfectly aligned. I combined my flowing energy with the Life-Shift Tools that I had already been using for myself and with my clients. I used my alpha energy to make a plan for determining how much money I would need and how I would go about earning it. I looked around at the resources I had, and created a strategy to enhance every aspect of my business: I would continue to motivate and help people manifest their dreams, but now on a larger scale. I would market my talent as a motivational speaker, including producing new inspirational CDs and tapes, and getting them distributed. I would continue to grow my seminar business and travel as much as I was physically able to do until the babies came.

I used my Focused Reflections to increase my magnetic energy, so that I could draw to me the people and opportunities to create the financial waterfall of abundance I needed. Every day I used my Power Prayers to hook into my Field of Love and communicate directly with this greater source. I spoke to my Dream Team, including my friends and family, about ways I needed to implement my new financial plan. I used their experiences to get the Goddess Repair Shop, a new aspect of my business, off the ground. I was asked to join the Anti-Aging Center in Westchester, and was appointed the head of the stress management department. With all these new responsibilities, I also wanted plenty of guidance for how to juggle it all and still end up with plenty of time to spend with my new babies. Three years later, the plan was starting to take shape, and I was beginning to see results. I was also pregnant. All my dreams were gloriously manifesting.

By the time the twins came, I was financially ready. Many of the aspects of my business strategy have worked, and others are still what I consider "works in progress." I can now afford to think seriously about a larger apartment. Most important, Francesca and Gian will have everything they need to feel loved and secure. I'm still working on building my dream further: Raising two children in a big city is like turning on a money vacuum! But I know that I will be able to overcome these financial challenges by using all of my resources together: my dynamic energy that makes me go after my dream every day and my magnetic energy that draws new opportunities to me. Together, I have been able to tap into the pure spiritual energy of my Field of Love that works through the magnetic and dynamic to make everything happen, revitalizing me as I overcome any obstacle in front of me.

The Energy of Money

Whatever your career dream is, I'm sure you want to make money at it. Think of money as energy. It is actually a force that goes from one person to the next. Just as there is money flowing out, there will always be money flowing in. There are times when I'm writing checks that it sure doesn't feel this way! But that's when I take a deep breath, surround the check with sparkling pink light, and write my Power Mantra "Return 100x," on the lower left corner of each check I make out—to send out a vibrational message to my Field of Love that the money I spend will return to me one hundredfold.

What stops money from flowing is the fear that it will disappear. Fear will cause you to hoard money and not take risks, stopping your energy—and your money—from circulating. The result is that you never feel like you have any money or can enjoy the pleasures of having it. And the economy doesn't get fed. Years ago, I had a client named Mina who had lived through the Depression.

Mina was terrified of putting her money in any investment that wasn't federally guaranteed. In fact, she preferred to keep a lot of her cash in a safe in her home. I could understand her inability to trust financial institutions, but her fear kept her from using her money wisely, so that it could generate more money that would have made her retirement more comfortable. Sometimes, even my clients who have a lot of money coming in are still terrified of spending it, living in fear that one day the money faucet will be turned off and it will stop flowing. I work with them to pinpoint where these fears are coming from and to change their belief systems about money.

The one thing about money is that there is an almost universal reaction to it. You can never have enough. When you experience true financial challenges, it is important that you don't allow yourself to surround your circumstances with additional fear; it will only block your energy so that you will be unable to use it to create the abundance that you need. Instead, work with my Focused Reflections on releasing fear and go back to Chapter 3 to empower and engage both your dynamic and magnetic energies so that you can begin drawing money toward you.

The following Focused Reflection has created dramatic results in my life and those of many of my clients when there was a need to shift out of money fear and into the energy of abundance.

Waterfall of Abundance

Do this exercise in a quiet space in your home, or as you're walking down the street, or sitting in your local coffee shop. Using the Whisper Breathing technique, relax, and patiently control your breath. Once you feel like your breath is flowing in freely and you are able to fill your lungs up with an abundance of oxygen, imagine yourself surrounded by the royal purple light of abundance that is flowing down like a waterfall from your Field of Love. Feel its nurturing energy permeating every cell of your body like a caressing touch. Imagine that above you there is a magnificent waterfall flowing with water or gold coins. Now imagine that this waterfall is pouring in through your head, infusing you with a feeling of abundance that is flowing through your body and out your toes. Use your magnetic energy and say "I open up to receive the abundance of the universe that is mine. Financial support easily flows into my life. I welcome it. I deserve it, and I am willing to receive it."

Are You Uncomfortable with Money?

Even if you have money, your own discomfort with having it can cause you to mismanage it, let it slip away, or work double time in order to get more. Money is a tool that allows us to do what we want to do. It is a powerful energy for supporting you as you work to manifest your dreams and desires. Why would you want to block it?

In my practice I find that one of the main blocks to allowing abundance to flow into our lives and/or enjoying it is guilt about having money. Some of my clients find that while they have money, they feel guilty about their wealth because so many others don't have it, including people who are close to them. They worry that they are taking money from someone else who is more deserving. They may also be holding on to negative judgments and beliefs about people who are rich as selfish, self-serving, and nasty to people who are less fortunate than they are.

There are many people out there who have the gift of wealth who fit that bill. But there are also just as many others who do not have money who act the same way. Money is not the culprit that turns people into nasty, greedy, heartless people. It only supports the tendencies that people have to begin with. I often suggest to these clients that they see money as spiritual energy in action. I have them think of ways that they can use their money for the benefit of humankind as well as enjoy the gift of having it. Once you believe that you deserve money, you will be able to draw it to you, enjoy it, and share it.

Be a Money Magnet!

You can take the first step toward drawing money and a great career opportunity toward you with the following exercise. This exercise engages your magnetic energy; so the more you do it, the more you'll be able to attract abundance to you.

Right now, think about what it would be like to have an unlimited amount of money. Picture what your life would look like and how different it would be from what you are experiencing now. Imagine how you would dynamically go about making this money and the steps you would need to take in order to fulfill this desire.

Close your eyes and visualize a spinning silver orb approximately one foot in front of your face. Breathe deeply, using your Belly Breathing technique, directing your breath into the silver orb. Feel as if you are a magnet drawing your money from the orb to yourself. Let go of any thoughts about or resistance to the impossibility of this, or feelings that you do not deserve this abundance. Let the good feelings of having what you want permeate every cell of your body, creating a sense of joy and well-being about having already received your heart's desires.

What's Blocking Your Abundance?

You might be thinking "Aleta, dreaming of a great job is one thing. Getting one is another." You're right. The hard work begins now. If you are experiencing a career setback, it's time to move on. Maybe you still enjoy key parts of your job, but your heart is telling you that there's a better opportunity, one that will connect you to your desires, help you create a new dream, and have more money so that you can pursue it. Maybe you've been out of the workplace for a long time. Or maybe you've always disliked your job but you didn't know what else to do, so you've remained stuck. Whatever your situation, I want to help you get past your fears about careers—and money. Then you can let the energies of creativity and prosperity flow into your life, fueling and financing your dreams.

Do you ever wonder why it is that if you hate your current job so much, you still don't leave? Or why the money you are making does not match your skill set or education level, or reflect the hard work you are putting in? Chances are that your energy is blocked, which is both holding you back and not letting the money flow in. Let's look at some of the most common blocks to determine what's been stopping you from reaching the abundant life that you deserve.

Money Block #1: "I Don't Deserve It"

We all deserve to fulfill our dreams. If you were able to break through your obstacles and receive support before, you can do it again. Do not let your fear of failure hold you back from trying. Maybe you never thought of yourself as an entrepreneur, or you think you couldn't possibly market yourself, or find office space, or be organized enough to run your own business. Maybe you think that you couldn't handle the cash flow problems that can crop up when there's no steady paycheck. Trust me, many of the self-employed women I know swore that they couldn't possibly do these things either. Now, they have released their fears and either mastered these skills or used their magnetic energy to draw in the people who can help them. They have hired accountants who can balance their checkbooks and do their taxes, editors who can proofread their marketing materials, and other professionals who can split the cost of office space. Everything is possible, and you deserve at least the chance to try.

The Litmus Test

Sit or stand in front of a mirror and look deeply into your eyes. Begin talking about your dream job, the amount of money you want to make, or a creative project you desire. Think about the excitement that you feel and the reasons why you deserve support to have it. If you see your pupils get smaller, it's because in your heart you do not believe that you deserve what you desire. If that is the case, take a deep breath and begin to repeat the following Power Mantras: "I deserve to have a job that I love and am excited about," "I deserve to be financially rewarded for my value," "I am talented and deserve to have the physical and financial support to manifest my creative projects." Repeat these mantras until you see the pupils of your eyes get bigger, showing that you are really starting to believe them. This might take many minutes, but don't stop. Push past any discomfort and just keep talking until you can see in your eyes that you believe.

Some of my clients do a simple version of this, looking into the mirror whenever they're in a bathroom, gazing into their eyes, and repeating their Power Mantra out loud or silently to themselves. A sticky note placed on the mirror is a good way to remind yourself to say your mantra. And a sticky note of the appropriate color—for instance, yellow for perseverance or royal purple for faith, trust, and belief—will remind you to use Color Immersion too. Look at your hot pink stickie, see yourself surrounded by a hot pink sun, and say "The more that I allow myself to receive, the more people will love and support me and the more I can give to others." Now, feel your magnetic energy drawing to you the job, career, creative project, or finances that you desire.

Money Block #2: Not Taking Responsibility for Creating What You Desire

You have to start your energy ball rolling to fulfill your dream. Some of my clients have stayed too long in a job because they were too much in their magnetic energy and kept waiting to get a raise, only to see other, "less-committed" employees walk away with bigger bonuses. These women thought that their good work would be noticed and they would be tapped for a promotion, and were surprised to find themselves passed over yet again. The business world is tough, and it isn't always fair. It's possible that you really don't belong in that job anymore, and the universe is sending a subtle message that maybe it's time to move on. If you find yourself in that situation, revisit Chapter 3 and work on the exercise that gets you connected to your dynamic energy, then work with your magnetic energy to draw a new situation to you.

Sometimes you need to be proactive to get what you want and deserve. And if you don't see it coming your way, then maybe it's time for a change. Take the risk and ask for what you want. The business world requires a bit more alpha energy than we've previously been discussing. But knowing when you need to be alpha, knowing when you need to be magnetic, and knowing when you have to balance both energies is what this book is really all about. In this case, you need to harness your dynamic energies in order to take your job, or your job search, to the next level. Then, using your Magnetic Feminine energies, set your best intention, watch it unfold, and feel like you are drawing it to you.

If you are planning to start fresh, here are some great alpha tasks you can do to get the process started:

✦ Talk to everyone you know about their jobs and why they love them or hate them.

- Talk to people in a different division of your company or who are in the same position as you are but at a different company.
- Go to job fairs.
- Take a course or invest in equipment and start doing what you love to do.
- Talk to other people who share your interests—and learn how they are fulfilling their dreams.
- Set specific goals for yourself, write them into your calendar in ink, and follow through with that dynamic can-do energy! These goals might be "Make five calls to potential employers this week," or "Get on the Internet and research this career," or "Volunteer to learn more about this career."
- Draw more people into your Dream Team who can help you. Check in with them regularly, reporting back on the progress you've made on your goals to discover and manifest your dream career.

Money Block #3: Should I Stay or Should I Go?

So many of my clients find themselves unsure about whether to stay in a job that's not working for them or leave for the unknown. Often, they are afraid to take the risk because they think they only have two choices: stay or go. But life is not like the old Chinese take-out menus, when you were allowed to pick a dish only from either column A or column B. Life is full of options. Even if you choose to stay in your job, there are at least two decisions you can still make to further your dream. You could:

Stay and fix the situation: Too often, women are afraid to speak up and ask for what they want. When you get in touch with your magnetic energy and feel deserving of what you need, it's much easier to draw on your dynamic energy, go into your boss's office, and ask! Maybe you need an assistant. Maybe you need to be spending less time in meetings or tied to the ever-ringing phone and more time generating new clients. Maybe you need to be better compensated for the work you are doing. Or maybe you have some ideas about how to make the workplace more efficient so that you don't feel drained from dealing with endless crises. Until you ask, you can't know if your employer will say no. If you think your job can be made deeply fulfilling just by having some key changes made, use what you learned in Chapter 5 to remove obstacles and bring in the transformative energies of courage and creativity, and try to make the situation work. If you succeed in making these changes, the feeling of empowerment will reinvigorate you. You might even start loving your job!

Stay . . . and prepare to go: When work is stressful, it's hard to imagine finding the energy to discreetly job hunt. But when you clear your blocks and balance your energies, you will find calmness and creativity, as well as the drive to put one foot out the door. For example, my client Christine was thrilled to land a job as an assistant to a famous fashion photographer. She loved photography so much that she didn't mind lugging his equipment here and there, setting up shoots, and spending hours doing paperwork.

Six months later, Christine was miserable. She'd always been interested in fashion, but she wasn't particularly interested in watching models pose a thousand ways in fifteen different outfits over the course of three hours. Much of the job was mind-numbing. Worse, her boss, who had initially lured her in with promises of teaching her everything he knew, was short-tempered and wouldn't take the time to answer her questions, let alone show her the ropes. When she began to complain to her friends and family, she heard her own fears echoed back to her: "You can't quit a job before a year is up. No one will hire you—they'll think you're unreliable," "How are you going to pay your bills if you quit?" and "You'll never get a better opportunity. Your boss is famous!"

Christine came to me in distress, saying, "I don't know what to do. I really hate fashion photography. I want to change my job, but I'm afraid I'm going to make the wrong decision."

I worked to help Christine let go of fearing the disapproval of her family and friends. I asked her to imagine what she would really want to do if anything was possible. I said, "Pretend you're in a darkroom about to develop the photo that captures the image of you as happy and successful in your career. As you look at the image in the developing tray, what are you seeing?"

Christine closed her eyes and was quiet for a little while. "It's an image of me, taking photographs. Now it is shifting to be an image of me framing my photographs for public display."

"Good," I said. "I want you to work with this image. See it surrounded in vibrant orange, and as you hold the picture in your mind, say the Power Mantra 'I am working toward my future in which I have the right and perfect job, feeling happy, fulfilled, and financially rewarded.' Now look deeper and tell me what else you see."

Christine thought for a moment, and said, "I'm framing photographs I've taken, and they're photos that really move people. I see people looking at them and being inspired." After a little while, Christine opened her eyes, and I asked her, "So, how can you go about making this dream into a reality?"

"Well," she responded, "I suppose a good start would be working with a photojournalist rather than a fashion photographer, and maybe getting out to shoot some rolls of my own. . . ."

"Great," I said, "I want you to tell me more. What do you need to do and whom do you need to contact to make those things happen? Now surround what you want in gold light."

"Right off the bat, I need to buy a new lens, and book some darkroom time. . . . I could also go to that exhibit of photographs that's at the Museum of Modern Art right now. That might inspire me."

I said, "That's great! Keep thinking of ways you can get more involved in photography and inspired. Write down names of photographers you admire and see if their photographs are in books you can take out from the library. And keep seeing that mental photograph of yourself snapping and framing fabulous photographs."

Christine stayed at her job, but began making the inquiries that were on her list. After a couple of weeks of working with her list, Christine called a photographer she admired to see if he needed an assistant, and he told her that he didn't, but maybe she would be interested in a job that was opening at a stock photo house. Christine got hired, and spent her days researching and sending out photographs that were truly extraordinary. Not long after she began her new job, she called me and said, "I'm so glad you supported me in leaving my old job—now I know what I really want to do: create photos that have the power to inspire people."

I knew that Christine had a lot of talent, and that if she left behind her bad situation to follow her desire, she would be successful. Today she is a famous photographer, traveling the world taking photographs for *National Geographic.*

Money Block #4: Afraid to Take Risks

I know that you'd like some assurance before you take that leap of faith into the unknown and start on the path to a new career, but life doesn't work that way. As you've learned, to manifest any desire, you need to jump in feetfirst and open yourself to the experience 100 percent. I'm not saying quit your day job immediately, but I am saying that every day, you should take at least one step forward. Then let your higher spiritual body guide you through the voice inside your heart. When you let go of your mental and emotional blocks, connect to your Field of Love, and bring in your magnetic and dynamic energies, opportunities and support will become available. You'll hear about jobs, you'll hook up with the right people, and money and resources will flow into your life because the universe will support you when you are on the path to your destiny.

But if you play it safe and stay put, you will not live your destiny. It's far better to let yourself envision a fulfilling career for yourself, put forth your best effort to achieve your desires and dreams, and not quite make it, than not to try at all. Even if your career success is limited or short-lived, you will never forget the joy of that experience. If you stay connected to that joy, you will know what your next move should be. Listen to your heart when it says "It's time to make a change."

If you take the leap of faith and boldly shift out of your comfort zone, you'll be energized and enthusiastic about your life. You will become comfortable doing what you have to do so that you can eventually do what it is you want to do.

Take the Plunge Energy Bath

To get yourself really keyed up to go for your new career and forget about the risks, try this invigorating bath. It will help you slough off all the dead skin cells and bring your energy up so that you'll be able to take the first necessary steps to your new financial future.

Fill the tub with warm water and soak for ten minutes without doing anything. Then, for the next ten minutes, use a body brush or loofah sponge and a mixture of half a cup of sea salt mixed with olive oil to exfoliate all of your skin. Put the mixture directly on the sponge and use a bit of pressure to rub it on your skin in a circular motion. Start at your feet and work your way up your body, including your face and scalp. As you are scrubbing away, say to yourself the following Power Mantras:

+ I am releasing all negative ideas about money. Money is the support I need to manifest my dream.
+ The more money I receive, the more I can give to others.
+ Money is spiritual energy in action.
+ When you are done, drain the water and rinse quickly with a cold splash.

Money Block #5: The Alarm Bell of Envy

We have all had the experience of feeling envious, even jealous, of someone we feel is more successful than we are. These negative thoughts come up when we feel that we could never achieve what they have done, so we downplay their successes with statements like, "She wasn't that beautiful before the enhancements," "I heard she's a bitch to work for," or "I can't believe *she* landed that husband."

While you may feel better by spreading the gossip, you could use your energy to create for yourself some of the things that you may envy. From now on, whenever you feel jealous, see it as an alarm bell going off to remind you that you can shift your energy and focus on what *you* want in *your* life rather than concentrating on what you envy in others. The following is a helpful exercise to do whenever you hear that alarm go off.

Shifting Out of Envy

Start focusing your breath, using your Relaxation Breathing. When you are relaxed, imagine that you are holding an emerald green ball of light in your left hand. Place your left hand on your heart center as you inhale, and breathe in the light. Ask yourself, "What am I feeling envious of?" Breathe and let the answers come up. Then ask yourself, "What is creating these feelings of envy? Do I feel inadequate because someone else's life seems to be better than mine? Am I focused on another's success while negating my own? Do I feel like I could never have what someone else has?"

If you answered yes to any of these questions, then you need to release your feelings of inadequacy, envy, and lack into the emerald green light as you exhale forcefully. Then ask yourself, "What makes me unique and valuable? What special talents and skills do I possess?" As you inhale, feel yourself receiving and acknowledging them. Allow yourself to be proud of your accomplishments and grateful for what you have created in your life. Hear the rushing sound of your spiritual body as it fills your physical, emotional, and mental bodies with its unconditional love, and ask yourself what you need to do to create happiness and the fulfillment of your desires, and then make a plan for how you are going to do it.

Curing the *What ifs*

As you think about pursuing your dream, any number of ugly *What if* questions will be sure to pop up once in a while to throw you off track: "What if I fail?" "What if I'm wrong?" "What if I'm not good enough?" As soon as these happen, reject them immediately. Turn those thoughts from "What if . . ." into "I am . . ." and "I can . . ."

My client Rick began cutting hair in a department-store beauty parlor in downtown Kansas City. Even though he didn't know a soul in New York, his dream was to move to Manhattan and open his own salon. Instead of asking himself, "What if I don't have the talent?" or "What if I can't gather the money to even get to New York City?" Rick kept telling himself, "I am a New York City hairstylist, and I am getting better every day" or "I can move to New York City. My own salon awaits me." It's no surprise that Rick now has his own very busy salon in Chelsea.

Rick also changed negative *What ifs . . .* into positive *What ifs. . . .* When he got to New York City he had to start at the bottom again, shampooing customers instead of cutting hair. Whenever he was elbow-deep in suds, he'd ask himself, "What if I got a loan from the small business association to start my salon?" "What if I bought the furniture secondhand, or took over an existing salon?" "What if I told my customers they could have a discount on their next cut or color if they bring me a new client, to generate more business?" When you turn the *What ifs* around to positive questions, you generate all sorts of creative solutions and options to help you realize your dreams.

Find Your Power

When you open yourself to respond to the calls from your soul and the waterfall of abundance that is available to you, you can make the most impossible career dream into a reality. Think of all the people whose great careers started with only a vision and a will, but who took the risks, went for it, and achieved their destinies. Whether it was a great singer who persevered against the odds, or a young man who believed that personal computers would change the lives of everyday people, or someone in your own life whose passion and commitment inspire you, many have found the courage and perseverance to life shift and walk the path of their destinies. Now that you know how to clear your blocks and engage your energy, there is nothing stopping you from attracting abundance and creating a fulfilling career.

Keep in mind, however, that money, fame, or even a great new job will not make us happy in itself. True happiness and a feeling of contentment come from the ability to harmonize our alpha and magnetic energies, build our internal Field of Love, feel the love that we have for ourselves, and then generate that outwardly in our relationships, work, and finances. Love, appreciation, and gratitude are the main energies that *attract* and help us *receive* success in our lives, which is measured by the amount of joy and fulfillment we experience.

What's more, lots of money and a great job won't even give you authentic, lasting personal power. This comes only when you get into your core energy: when you've balanced your Magnetic Feminine with your dynamic, and when you are in your highest spiritual self. When this occurs, you feel a kind of self-reliance internally as well as externally. You will be able to draw on the support of others, as well as give of yourself and your newfound abundance in the spirit of mutual support. You will be amazed by the joy and fulfillment you will feel living the life you've dreamed of.

EPILOGUE

New York City, February 2005

If you had met me a year ago, you might not even recognize me today. For that matter, you wouldn't recognize my apartment either.

So much of what I used to do and how I used to be is no more. I barely have time to take a shower, my roots are perpetually showing, and I haven't had a manicure in months. My twins are decked out in their fabulous little baby outfits and I'm walking around in sweats. I used to have a manicure every week. And once upon a time, I really loved beautiful clothes.

I've had the same apartment for twenty-five years, and it used to also function as my office and studio. Now it looks like a baby warehouse. Wall to wall, it's filled with baby toys, swings, car seats, strollers, and bottles. A big bear hangs over the babies' crib in place of the Buddha head that used to be there.

But I'm certainly not complaining.

On April 17, my babies were christened at St. Paul the Apostle Church, just a few blocks from my home, in midtown Manhattan. This was the same church I would visit by myself to pray for the babies to be born.

Epilogue

The twins were adorned in white christening gowns with appropriate shoes and hats. However, the most touching part of the ceremony for me and, I was told, for others, was when I had my mother, father, and each of the four primary and twenty-six secondary godparents give their own blessing to Gian and Francesca, in addition to Father Paddack's, with the words "My gift to you is. . . ." This group of amazing friends spoke from their hearts, giving my children the gifts of creativity, laughter, love, loyalty, education, travel, and samba lessons.

My dream came true. Holding my babies at their baptism was the purest example of visualization, manifestation, and support I have experienced in my life. I had to create them in my mind before I could bring them to life.

So many people think that having babies after all those years spent happily being a free spirit must overwhelm me. That just hasn't happened. Instead, when I think of these two little beings who share my life, it makes me energized, joyful, and fulfilled. Honestly, at this age, you have to really want children.

The great gift of my children is the new beginning they have given me. At fifty-seven, I finally have my own family. A whole new world is opening up for me at a time when some people might believe I should be winding down. My life is no longer about nights out at my favorite restaurant, Bello's, followed by an evening at the theater. I haven't seen the inside of a gym in far too long. If my friends want to see me, they have to come to me—and I'll probably have a baby in my lap.

The twins have very different personalities, even from their earliest infancy, though they still detonate at precisely the same time. Gian is the more serious, Renaissance baby. He's very alert to music and anything visual. He also carries on baby conversations with the people who hold him and, of course, with his sister. He's very sensitive; he's got an almost telepathic energy. Gian senses when you're going to leave the room, and tears well up—it's as if you stabbed him in the heart. Francesca is a little more easygoing and a little more carefree. She has a penetrating gaze,

Epilogue

quietly observing everything around her. She laughs all the time and she loves to dance, as much as a baby can dance, kicking her legs vigorously to the music. They sometimes get competitive—especially Gian. When Francesca's diaper is being changed, Gian wants attention. Francesca doesn't care as much. She'll let Gian have the attention, being the older and more mature one, having arrived a full minute before her brother. Lately, they reach out and hold hands, looking at each other intently, cooing and smiling.

I love what little folk heroes the twins are around my neighborhood. People on the street stop and ask me how they're doing. The people in the deli, the cleaners, and the florist shop all ask, and I pull out the pictures. It's like this little village in the middle of Manhattan.

If there's any one thing I hope you will take away from my story, it's the idea that it is never too late to march to the beat of your own drummer. It's never too late to realize your passion and go for your dream by setting your own course. It's never too late to let go of what other people think. It's never too late to be true to yourself.

Someone asked me what I've learned from my babies. I said, What I've learned is something I thought I already understood. Just be in the moment, hold strong to your vision, have faith . . . and never give up. It's the best way I know of to give birth to your dreams.

ACKNOWLEDGMENTS

I've had many challenges in my life, but writing a book was by far the most daunting. So it is with immense gratitude and appreciation that I offer my thanks to the following amazing spirits who were there with me every step of the way to bring my message and the power of my work to you. Without their generous outpouring of creative talent and insightful suggestions, this book would not be nearly as rich and authentic.

I would like to extend my heartfelt thanks to all of those who have provided their love and support: My publicist, Heidi Krupp, is an amazing woman who got the ball rolling when she said in no uncertain terms, "You have to write a book." Nancy Hancock is my brilliant editor, who passionately nurtured the book from a single sheet of paper to the end. All the dedicated people at Simon & Schuster were terrific throughout the entire process. My enthusiastic agent, Matthew Guma, kept things logical, steady, and in perspective. My friend Arthur, who always had a bond of understanding that bridged time and who was there at the birth as my support and lifeline and always called to check in to see how I was doing. My multitalented assistant, Josie McGee, helped me with my writing deadlines while juggling babies. Nancy Pesky offered her expertise and guidance during the first stages of the book. Thanks to Pamela Liflander for her ability to jump in at the last minute with amazing organizational skills, clarity, a steady hand, and the collaborative vision to help birth the book; my fertility specialist, Dr. Jane Miller, who agreed to embark on this incredible journey with me, despite my age—she was always relentlessly positive about my chances of becoming pregnant. And thanks to Dr. Scher, whose loving expertise, support, reassurance, and enthusiasm were key factors in the success of my pregnancy. And none of this could have happened without Edna Deiparine, whose faithful and unwavering care for my children has made it all possible.

Thank-yous are also sent to my longtime friends Corrado De Genoa and Pam Lange, who sat for endless hours reading drafts of the manuscript. Dana Kennedy taught me to write about the truth. Chris Dennis and Brenda Earl De Paola are two women who not only contributed creatively but offered practical business advice as well. Mitch Suss, Alfred Brown, Gigi Jordan, Brigitte Britton, and Rita Christman were always there for me. My friends Cynthia Sullo and Caroline Nation could always make me laugh. Debbie Cohen and Barbara Pizik offered never-ending help with my professional wardrobe, and my very talented photographer, Ken Nahome, captured the essence of my work for the book cover. I'd also like to thank Denise Johnston and Georgia Malone for graciously offering their summer homes as writing retreats.

This book could not have been written without my Goddess Support Group: Lisa Marino, Linda Rucco, Lauren Martin, Kasey Cunningham, Jennifer Gahan, Erika Morrell, Rebecca Spence, and Candace Lazarus, who each took the time to offer their feedback and suggestions during the writing process. There were also wonderful energy workers and gifted colleagues who kept things flowing: Stuart Perrin, Housneau Onaran, Bill Touvert, Master Lee, and Siva Baba for their spiritual energy work; Sally Kravich, Jonny Bowden, Dr. Fredric Vagnini, and Dr. Lionel Bissoon for their nutritional counseling; Yamuna Zake, Lisa Avellino, and Lois Barth for keeping my body together; Joelle Dunrovich for always making sure my hair was ready for prime time; and Leda Serrey, Joe Wilson, and Giselle Terry for their brilliant forecasting.

I would like to specifically thank the extraordinary people and teachings that have impacted my work: E. 15 Acting School in London for igniting my creativity; Thurman Scott for skillfully guiding me through and teaching me emotional release work; the Actualism Center for its amazing light work; Monica Sands for a true experience of Tibetan Meditation and American Yoga; and Connie Neuton, a true, dedicated light being on this planet who taught and continues to teach me the power of Integrated Awareness.

Last, I would like to thank my family. My sister, Maria—journalist, human rights activist, and my biggest cheerleader—I love you. My brother, Curtis, his wife, Mary, and little Anthony Chester were a constant source of unending family support, as was my muse, my beloved cousin Jimmy Lonigro. And special thanks go to my godmother, Aunt Mary, who always told me to go for my dreams.

INDEX

Index

Index

Index

Index

Index

exercises (*cont.*)
   Red Light Connection, 218
   Release and Forgive, 174–75
   Release the Day, 26
   Releasing Feelings of Abandonment, 196
   Releasing to the Heavens, 155
   Revealing Your Desires, 8
   Rev Your Engine, 206
   Sensual Delights, 204–5
   shaman breathing, 78
   Shame Release, 217
   Shifting Out of Envy, 239
   Tantric Energy Circle, 220–21
   Temple of Transformation, 132–33
   What You Had, What You Deserve, 196
   What Your Gut Knows, 58
exhaustion, transformation of, xiv–xv
eye contact:
   in Reconnecting Through Releasing,
     190–91
   in Tantric Energy Circle, 220–21

failure:
   fear of, 230
   feelings of, xiii, 96, 118
faith, xiii, xv, 38, 104, 178, 231
   financial abundance and careers and, 231,
     237
   hopelessness transformed into, 122–25,
     132–33
   loss of, 15, 178
   transforming obstacles and, 108, 122–26,
     132–33
family, 109
   anger and, 88, 92
   self-love and, 167
   sex and, 200
   support from, xvii, 2–3, 61, 135–36
   see also children; fathers; mothers,
     motherhood; parents
fantasies, sexual, 211–12
fashion photography, 234–35
fathers, xii, 144
   of author, 1, 88, 107, 108, 121, 163, 164,
     198–99, 243
fatigue, 47, 74, 79
   chronic syndrome of, 126–27
   sex and, 200, 206
fear, 4, 20, 42, 75, 89, 159
   of abandonment, 168, 172, 194–96
   anger as cover for, 92
   of being hurt, 214–16

body's memory of, 28–29
of career change, 235
Color Immersion and, 35–38
defined, 112–13
of disappointing others, xviii, 1
energy blocks created by, 17, 24, 77, 98, 172
exercises for transformation of, 115–17
of failure, 230
of future, xviii
of inadequacy, 4, 9
instilled by mothers, 16, 17
letting go of, 3, 17, 91, 110, 115–17
love and romantic relationships and, 166,
   169
of money shortage, 11, 225–26
negative desire and, 10–11
as obstacle, 109
of parasites, 107, 108
of pursuit of dreams, xviii, 15, 16, 17
of rejection, 96, 144, 157
relationship choices based on, 166
release of, 26, 37, 108, 194, 195
of risk taking, 225, 233, 237–38
transformed into courage, 112–17,
   132–33
feminine:
   reintegration of, xiii
   see also magnetism, Magnetic Feminine
fennel oil, 40
fertility rituals, x, 72, 105–8
   in India, x, 105–8
fiber, dietary, 81
Field of Love, 102–4, 108, 112, 125, 170,
   196
   financial abundance and careers and, 224,
     225, 227, 237, 241
   other names for, 102
   sex and, 202
financial abundance, xv, xviii, 223–41
   blocking of, *see* money blocks
   dream of, 12
   Focused Reflections and, 224, 226, 227
   Power Mantras and, 225, 231, 235, 238
   see also money
financial support, 165, 174
Fire Letter, 116–17
fish, 80
focus, xv, 25, 53, 54
   on lacks, 99
   on pain vs. emotion, 90
   problems with, 16
   transforming obstacles and, 128, 130–34

Index

Index

Index

Index

Index

Index

physical self, physical energy (*cont.*)
  love note to, 85–86
  mental body vs., 207–9
  self-love and, 166, 170, 171
  sex and, 201–9
  spiritual body and, 98, 170, 171, 239
pink, pink light, 56, 93, 184, 225, 231
  gratitude and, 38, 121, 141, 142
  sex and, 204
  transformative powers of, 38
pleasing others, 1–2, 18, 51
pleasure, momentary, 11
political work, 20
positive attitude, 76
positive desires:
  defined, 8–9
  indicators of, 9
  shifting to, 11, 12
positive energies, xvii, 38, 95, 109
  blocking of, 91
  Power Mantras and, 41, 42
positive things, absorption of, 26
possibilities, regrets transformed into, 121–22
poverty, fear of, 11
power, 91
  expectation of, 42
  personal, 12, 36, 240–41
  of words, 95–96
powerlessness, 36, 44, 89
Power Mantras, 29, 41–43, 67, 178, 195
  designing your own, 42–43
  examples of, 42
  financial abundance and careers and, 225,
    231, 235, 238
  "God, God, only God," 102
  for love and romance, 184
  negative, 158
  for overcoming the monkey mind, 96–98
  sex and, 208, 213, 215, 219
  for support, 146, 148, 157
  That's for Me!, 118–19
  for transforming fear, 115
  for transforming obstacles, 112, 115,
    117–22, 125, 127, 129, 133
Power Prayers, 43–46, 224
  to connect with spiritual body, 101–2, 104
  Release and Transform, 129–30
  thank-you, 45–46, 197
practical, being, 18
prayers, 49, 148
  of intention, 108
  see also Power Prayers

pregnancy and childbirth, 52
  of author, ix–xi, xiii–xiv, xv, 3, 15, 49, 61,
    72, 74, 79, 80, 86, 135–38, 223–25
present tense, Power Mantras in, 42–43
problem solving, 159
protein, 78, 79
Pulling in the Energy Cord, 160
purple, 38, 128, 173, 204, 227, 231
  violet, 21–22, 213
purpose:
  question of, 18–19
  see also destiny

Quick Detox Workout, 84
Quick Water Detox, 82

rage, emotional wounds and, 89
Rameswaram ("water temple"), 107–8, 129
rape, 216
real estate, 66–67
receptivity, receiving, xiii, 38, 52, 54
  believing and, 64–66
  release and, 23–26
  shifting from false spirituality to
    appreciating the gift of, 138–44
  see also magnetism, Magnetic Feminine
reciprocity, lack of, 52
Reconnecting Through Releasing, 190–91
red, ruby, 35–36, 218, 220–21
Red Light Connection, 218
regrets, 110, 113
  release of, 108
  transformed into possibilities, 121–22,
    132–33
rejection, feelings of, 88, 89, 91
  Color Immersion and, 35, 36–37
  fear of, 96, 144, 157
  support and, 138–39
relationships, xv
  bad choices for, 166
  color and, 36, 37
  communication problems in, 90–91
  energy-draining, 130–31
  improvement of, 88
  loss of, x, 11, 37, 109, 122, 140, 164, 193–96
  loss of interest in, 51
  see also friends, friendships; love, loving
    relationships; romantic relationships
relaxation:
  Belly Breathing and, 31–32
  Energy Baths and, 40
Relaxation Breathing, 153, 174, 239

Index

Index

Index

Siva Baba, 105, 106
skin, 84
sleep, breathing and, 31
Sliwa, Curtis, 58, 114, 163
smoking, 47–48
social work, 20
solar plexus, 36, 101, 115, 160
soul mates, 165, 186–87
Southeast Asia, tsunami in, 18
spiritual self, spiritual energy, xiv, xvii, 15,
    73–77, 86, 98–104
    chakra for, 37
    destiny and, 20
    experience of connecting to, 99–101
    false, appreciating the gifts of giving and
        receiving vs., 138–44
    Field of Love and, 102–4, 225, 237
    financial abundance and careers and, 237,
        239
    as "light body," 98
    love and, 116–17, 194, 217, 239
    money as, 228
    opening to the, 171
    Power Prayers and, 43–45, 101–2, 104
    relationships and, 165, 166, 169–71, 174–77,
        194
    revelation of, xvi
    self-love and, 166, 169–71
    sex and, 202, 217–22
    transforming hopelessness and, 123, 125
stress, xv, 51, 77
    emotional effects of, 89
    job, 5
    old traumas and fears remembered
        during, 29
    release of, 8
stress hormones, 74
stroke, 83
subconscious mind, 95
success, xii, xiii, 150, 241
    as best revenge, 11–12
    career, 110–11
    expectations of, 42
    personal measures of, 23
    social definition of, 18
Sudan, slave trade in, 114
sugar, refined, 79, 80
support, receiving, xvii, 46, 53, 135–62
    blocking of, 136–37, 148–49
    Chat Room of Discontent and, 158–59, 197
    Circle of Giving and Receiving and, 141–42
    Dream Team and, 150–51, 155–58, 161

    exploding your obstacles and, 148–50
    from family, xvii, 2–3, 61, 135–36
    financial abundance and careers and, 231,
        237
    from friends, x, xvii, 61, 135, 136, 197
    giving too much vs., 159–60
    Gold Explosion and, 149–50
    from higher power, 37, 42, 108, 174
    It's All About You and, 143
    learning to trust other people and the
        universe for, 147–48
    letting go and moving on to, 151–55
    love and romance and, 165, 169, 170
    mutual, shifting from feeling indebted to,
        137–38
    shift from distrust to, 145–47
    shift from perfectionism to accepting
        others' limitations and, 144–45
    shifting from false spirituality to
        appreciating the gifts of giving and
        receiving, 138–44
    from spiritual body, 169–71, 194
    from universal energy, 110

tailbone, 35–36, 171, 220
Take the Plunge Energy Bath, 238
Tantric Energy Circle, 220–21
tape-recording, of Focused Reflections, 34
tea, green, 82
teachers, 20
telephone calls, intuition about, 58
television watching, 51
Temple of Karnak, 35
Temple of Transformation, 132–33
tensions, release of, 26, 27–28, 40–41
Thanksgiving, 96–97
thank-you prayers, 45–46, 197
That's for Me!, 118–19
theater group, community, 145–46
thinking, thought, see mental self, mental
    energy
thoughtfulness, 154
throat, as energy center, 37
Tibetans, 9
Time to Let Go, 193
touch, sense of, 203, 204, 210–11
toxins, removal of:
    breathing and, 77–78
    colors and, 34
    connecting the Four Bodies and, xvii, 46,
        77–78, 80–82, 89–97, 103
    emotional, 89–94, 201

Index

ABOUT THE AUTHOR

*T*he words *healer* and *success coach* don't do justice to Aleta St. James. Her energy comes through her beauty, wit, and elegance. She is not your typical New Age mystic. A former successful actress and director, Aleta's own struggles with the emotional roller coaster of show business led her on a journey of personal healing and self-discovery. She began studying Tibetan meditation, Bioenergetics, healing with light, and integrated awareness. To her surprise, she found that these techniques, combined with her intuitive gifts that began in childhood, could help heal and empower others. And a new career was born.

The system Aleta developed, known as "Energy Transformations," is a powerful combination of practical tools and healing techniques that she has developed over years of study with some of the great spiritual masters and teachers from around the world. Her life-shifting techniques became so in demand that she began traveling internationally, giving lectures, private seminars, and hands-on private sessions. Today, her clientele includes celebrities from the fashion, film, and music industries, sports and TV personalities, as well as CEOs and people from all walks of life.

She became a true example of the power of her own work when she delivered twins in her late fifties, confirming her most basic belief: There is no such thing as an impossible dream. With the birth of her twins, as more and more women came to Aleta seeking help in becoming pregnant, she saw how challenging fertility issues can be for so many women. Aleta combined forces with Dr. Ming Jin, an authority in the field of Chinese medicine who specializes in infertility treatment, to create a holistic fertility center to help women manifest their dreams of motherhood.

Aleta is dedicated to helping women stay young, vibrant, and beautiful from the inside and out, with her Goddess Repair Shop, featuring the latest in antiaging technology. She is the creator and director of the Anti-Stress Programs at the Focus 28 center in New York.

To learn more about Aleta's upcoming events, seminars, and Internet conferences, go to www.aletastjames.com.